WORDS OF PEACE
IN NATIVE LAND

Editor: Agnès Saint-Laurent
Reviser: Carmine Starnino
Proofreader: Elizabeth Lewis
Graphic Design: Chantal Landry

EXCLUSIVE DISTRIBUTOR:

For Canada and the United States:
Simon & Schuster Canada
166 King Street East, Suite 300
Toronto, ON M5A 1J3
phone: (647) 427-8882
    1-800-387-0446
Fax: (647) 430-9446
simonandschuster.ca

Catalogue data available from Bibliothèque
et Archives nationales du Québec

Cliche, Guylaine, 1969-

03-16

© 2016, Juniper Publishing,
division of the Sogides Group Inc.,
a subsidiary of Québecor Média Inc.
(Montreal, Quebec)

Legal deposit: 2016
National Library of Québec
National Library of Canada

ISBN 978-1-988002-56-9

Conseil des Arts   Canada Council
du Canada   for the Arts

We gratefully acknowledge the support of the Canada Council
for the Arts for its publishing program.

We acknowledge the financial support of the Government
of Canada through the Canada Book Fund for our publishing
activities.

GUYLAINE CLICHE
AND THE **MOHAWK TRADITIONAL**
COUNCIL OF KAHNAWAKE

WORDS OF PEACE
IN NATIVE LAND

Mohawk Culture, Values and Traditions

JUNIPER
PUBLISHING
A Quebecor Media Corporation

To all our mothers who have ever fulfilled the role of Female Chief and to all the faces yet beneath the Earth who must rise to fill the role of Female Chief.

 STUART MYIOW JUNIOR

Returning to the Great Circle of Life

For millions of years, the interdependence of the diversity of living species has allowed the world to exist in a harmony that has flowed through the continuum of time. This diversity of species has nurtured the world and kept all the natural systems in balance.

Humanity emerged and, after hundreds of thousands of years, hominids evolved into what we are today, living happily within the Circle of Life. We took from it, and we gave back to it, and thus humanity—sharing the world with the others without thought of domination—was a part of this wondrous biocentric reality.

Unfortunately, human evolution took an abrupt turn toward the dark side with the emergence of anthropocentrism: the view that humans are superior and are the *all-important centre of Creation*. From that moment, the anthropocentric human began to take from nature without respect and without giving back.

Anthropocentrism, this sickness of the human soul, burst upon the natural world in an aggressive form of dominance: exploiting nature with impunity; exterminating and enslaving entire species of plants and animals; ruthlessly vanquishing all peoples who resisted what the anthropocentric human referred to as a manifest destiny.

Indigenous human communities that resisted this violent anthropocentric force were persecuted, exterminated and set aside, as if they were irrelevant to the dictated *superiority* of humankind over all other species.

The once universal position of humanity as a part of the Circle of Life has been viciously replaced with this proclamation of humanity as the dominant species controlling all other forms of life.

Anthropocentrism is the proclamation of the dark side of humanity that demands subservience from all other forms of life and obedience from all indigenous societies that struggle to keep the flame of biocentrism burning.

But as long as that flame still flickers, there is hope for humanity.

The explosion of anthropocentric dominance now threatens life on every part of this planet, to the extent that we have entered a new era now called the Anthropocene.

The Anthropocene is the sixth major extinction the planet has experienced, the last being the Jurassic period 65.2 million years ago.

Massive species extinction, the poisoning of the soil and the water, the acidification of the ocean, the rising levels of greenhouse gases and the out-of-balance escalating populations of human beings represent the disheartening result of the Antropocene.

We live in a world of 7.5 billion humans, growing at a rate of a billion plus every decade. To continue this insane growth we slaughter 65 billion animals raised without respect and whose flesh we eat without empathy or consciousness. The Yanomami* refer to the dominant paradigm as the *termite people* gobbling up the world because we are stealing the carrying capacity of eco-systems and thus diminishing the great Circle of Life.

---

*. The Yanomami are a group of indigenous people who live in the Amazon rainforest on the border between Venezuela and Brazil.

If humanity is to survive, we will have to shake off the mantle of anthropocentrism and return to living in harmony and respect with the plants and animals of the world.

This will happen or humanity will perish because no species can survive outside of the great Circle of Life.

To return to this Circle we will need guidance and that guidance can only come from the few who still embrace the understanding that we are a part of the great Circle and not outside of it.

In 2006, I spoke with some representatives of the Mohawk Traditional Council in Ottawa, and, in 2007, I had the great honour to be presented with the flag of the Five Nations when some of my crew and I visited the Mohawk of Kahnawake.

The flag of the Five Nations flies from the masthead of our Sea Shepherd Conservation Society ships along with the flags presented to us by Aboriginal tribes in Australia and the Maori in Aotearoa.

These flags symbolize our link with the biocentric understanding of indigenous people throughout the world who collectively carry the sacred truth that we must never lose: *To survive, humanity must return within the Circle of Life. We must humble ourselves to share this beautiful planet with all of our relations of every species of plant and animal.*

In my work with marine conservation I never lose sight of the fact that hope lies in the flame that indigenous biocentric communities keep burning. I see that light through the haze of human greed and selfishness and I see the promise of that flame guiding us toward a future where we will return to harmony with the natural world.

Toward that end I keep in mind this Iroquois mantra: that we must never make any decision in our lives unless we take into account the consequences of that decision on all future generations.

 CAPTAIN PAUL WATSON

Ne Shennen, Ne Kariwiio, Ne Kasatensara - Peace, Prosperity, Power and Equality to All

Five Nation Longhouse Confederacy

Ka-nin-ke-a-ka - People of the Flint

KAHNAWAKE KANIEN'KEHÁ:KA NATION

Ohenton Kariwatehkwen
Before All Else

Whenever the united Chiefs of the Great Peace shall assemble for the purpose of holding Council, the Onontake Chiefs shall open it by expressing their gratitude to their cousin Chiefs. In greeting them, they shall address and offer thanks to Sky Woman, the first being in the physical world; our Grandmother Moon, the beating heart of our Mother Earth; our Mother Earth where people dwell; and to all the Women from the youngest to the eldest as they are the Mothers of our Nations; to the streams of water, to the pools and the lakes and all the life that lives within; to the Corn, Bean and Squash, the Three Sisters of sustenance; to the fruits; to the medicinal plants; to the forest trees for their usefulness; to the animals that serve as food and give their pelts for clothing; to the great winds and the lesser winds; to our Grandfathers the Thunders; to our Eldest Brother the Sun, the Mighty Warrior; to the winged creatures that live upon the winds, those messengers of life that reveal the Creator's wishes; and to the Great Creator that dwells in all things, giving all things useful to the united people, and is the source and ruler of all health and life.

Tsitewaterah'kwaketskwas Kanhhóa
Eastern Door

Imagine a fire and people sitting peacefully around it.
Imagine the joy of children playing. Imagine the wind that
carries the scent of the surrounding vegetation, the sage who
smokes, the eagles that fly, wheeling, in the belly of the sky.
Imagine the circle opening to let you sit.

Guylaine Cliche

Plumes d'Aigles
Eagle Feathers

As a farmer's child, I grew up in the countryside, in Sainte-Catherine-de-Hatley. From a young age, I learned the language of the sky, animals and forest, thanks to my parents who were able to interpret nature. We knew, for example, if it was going to rain the next day, from the colour and texture of the sunset; or what type of winter we were to have, according to the peels of the onion that we harvested. It is in this context that I have had the privilege to immerse myself in the Earth's beauty. Make no mistake, though: I went through many difficulties after my childhood—a chaotic adolescence that led me to a difficult start as a woman: single parenting and poverty. All this prepared me to accomplish with courage what I am doing today.

In July 2014, the youngest of my three sons left the nest. A mother at 18 and a single parent for most of my life since then, I had attained, by this stage, a sense of accomplishment. Because I did not need the spacious apartment which we occupied, I moved out at the same time as my son.

One afternoon when I was putting the finishing touches to my move, a friend came to give me a gift: two eagle feathers, a black and a white one. The carcass of the bird had been fished out of the Saint-Francois River by the father of this friend. Having collected feathers for a long time, this gift represented to me an omen. I realized that the Spirit of the Eagle would guide my steps in my new life.

Once the move was completed, I wanted to celebrate my new home and I asked a woman of indigenous origin to do a ceremony with the feathers that I had received. When she heard they were from an eagle she reacted strongly and wanted to teach me the Eagle medicine[1].

I followed her recommendations for a few days until I started to feel suffocated. In fact, she called me every day, claiming to have received messages from the eagle, and sometimes very early in the morning, before I got out of bed. She even accused me of having betrayed her, because I went to honor the carcass of the eagle without her. I could not remain under the guidance of a woman who, on behalf of the Eagle's teachings, tried to maintain a domineering authority over me. I released myself from her grip, knowing that an eagle does not live in a cage.

In August, I went to the International Day of Indigenous Peoples at the Botanical Garden of Montréal, where I met members of the Mohawk Traditional Council of Kahnawake[2]. I was particularly moved by the teachings of Stuart Myiow Junior, Secretary of the Council and I felt that this encounter would be decisive for the rest of my life.

Stuart spoke about current global challenges. When he said we have to reach 7 billion people as soon as possible, I felt concerned. As I'm an author, I thought I could participate in this goal by sharing the teachings of the Traditional Council in a book. After the ceremony at the Garden, I spoke with Stuart, but didn't mention my idea. He asked me to leave my contact information with Edith, the group's translator.

That night, some members of the Council were doing a Full Moon Ceremony on Mont-Royal. Everyone was invited. I opted not to go, because I had to return home, an hour-and-a-half drive away, and I also wanted to take advantage of my stay in Montréal to visit a friend.

---

1. Medicines include everything that bring healing (plants, location, people, etc.)
2. Native reserve (Mohawk) in suburban Montreal

Once at my friend's house, I was not at peace. I felt an inner call: Go to the ceremony. I gave in and headed over to Mont-Royal without knowing exactly in which direction to go. Was the ceremony occuring at the summit? In the forest? I did not know, but I was connected to my intuition and ordered my mind to obey. I walked toward the path that would lead me to the top of the mountain. I asked people, but nobody knew where the ceremony was being held. The light was fading quickly, and I soon found myself alone in the dark of the forest. Marijuana smells and creaking noises gave me a cold sweat . . . and confirmed that I was less alone than I thought. I told myself a hundred times that I was crazy to have entered the woods of Montréal at the beginning of the night. When I almost reached the top, I was despondent. It was dark for a while now and I had to turn back through this dissuasive darkness.

Coming out of the woods, I was disappointed not to have found the group but I was relieved to finally see the lights of Montreal. Suddenly, I heard "Guylaine!" Edith was standing right in front of me. An apparition, it seemed so this coincidence destabilized me. I had arrived at the exact location of my quest, just in time to take part in the ceremony. Considering how huge an area Mont-Royal covers, it was beyond coincidence that I would arrive at that exact place, at that exact time.

The sacred fire was burning, and gathered around it were those who came to share their intentions, their gratitude, and their love with Grandmother Moon. First, sage and tobacco circulated. Finally the speaking feather went around so that we could all express ourselves. I had always been fascinated by the Moon and I felt that I was exactly where I needed to be, among those I needed to meet.

Back home, comfortable in my bed, I could not sleep before very late in the night. I kept thinking over the events of the day. I knew this story was just beginning.

In the days that followed, I stayed in contact with some members of the Traditional Council, but I did not speak about the book yet. I first contacted my editor at Sogides Group who expressed interest in my idea. I then met the Council who granted me their trust and agreed to launch the project.

Then in September, a few days after my first visit to the Kahnawake reserve, I joined the people of the Longhouse in a rally near Ottawa, where people from different nations gathered for a weekend at Grandmother Aki Songideye Ikwe's place. Several circles and teachings took place in order to honor and respect our Mother Earth and the life she carries. The dances, ceremonies, and the sacred fire that burned day and night under the care of its Guardian unsettled and reassured me at the same time. I found my *landmarks* when I stopped resisting mentally. I had the sensation of emerging from a long lethargy. It appeared obvious to me that I was starting a process that would transform me irreversibly.

Ordinary contact with the people of the Longhouse is a teaching in itself. The most significant lessons aren't transmitted orally but through experience. For example, in my first meeting in Kahnawake, I acted as most people do: I tried to intervene, approve, when Stuart spoke to me. He stared back without reaction and continued to speak as if he had not heard me. That was how I learned silence. Nobody explained it to me. In a circle, the one that holds the feather speaks and the others listen without, in any way, interrupting until everyone has spoken. A large circle can easily last for half a day.

The way the Mohawks live and communicate, their vision of life, transforms everyone who frequents them, and it's important to accept that we won't understand everything right away. Sometimes something happens and you won't fully grasp its meaning until other events occur, leading to the formation of a complete thought or a clear sentiment. This is also a key to reading this book.

I always find it difficult to leave the Longhouse and return home to non-Natives. I've come to realize how much we tune out and interrupt each other. We put more energy in preparing our response than absorbing the words being said. Since meeting the Natives, I've become intolerant of those who fail to listen when it's my turn to speak. Among First Nations, and now in my heart, speech is sacred.

One day, in a group, I tried to explain how to get to the Longhouse but everyone was talking over me. Then, I shared with them my learning of the speech. Someone replied that I was lucky to know how to keep silent when someone talks, and added that it is because I frequent the Mohawks that I am that way.

Later that day we were all gathered around the fire, at Kahnawake, for the Raspberry Ceremony. I had sufficient distance from what that person told me to be able to share my comprehension of the situation with the people around the circle: My ability to silently listen when someone speaks doesn't come from the Mohawks. It's a trait I already possessed—my contact with the Mohawks simply woke it up. This has always been part of my identity. And the reason my identity has come to life with the Mohawk is because they themselves are firmly anchored in their own identity.

Every time I go to Kahnawake, I come to learn something not necessarily from them, but generally about myself. My reactions to what I see, hear and experience with the Mohawk are the essential teachings that lead me to deploy my own identity. I am White. I will not become Mohawk. The more I am connected to who I am, the more I will be in harmony with them.

By reading this book, you will enter into a speaking circle. Within, 15 individuals from 9 different roots express themselves (Mohawk, Innu, Anishnabe, Kabyle, Zapotec, Irish, American, Québécois, and Jewish). All these people share the same vision, regardless of their origin: to preserve life by protecting our Mother Earth. In order to respect the speech of everyone, the writing work has been accomplished in respecting the way they talk or express themselves in orality.

The content of this book was collected in the course of several meetings, spread over an entire year. It is fully approved by the Mohawk Traditional Council of Kahnawake, and central among their traditional teachings is the Moon Teaching. Since this teaching is the heart of the book, its structure is built like a lunar cycle. There are 28 days between the New Moon and the Last Quarter, so the book contains 28 chapters divided into 4 phases (New Moon,

First Quarter, Full Moon, Last Quarter). In addition, at the end of the book, there is a glossary where all allophone words are listed. Chapter titles and speaker names are in the original language of the person who holds the speaking feather, and they are subtitled in English. And finally, at the beginning of each chapter, the *Kanienke'ha'ka* (Mohawks) are represented by three feathers that point upwards, since this is the way they wear them.

Furthermore, to understand the issues of this book, we should not confuse band council[3] with traditional council. Band council is a colonial political system imposed on the Native people assimilating them to non-Native identity. Traditional council handles the matrilineal constitution that unites politics and spirituality.

When I talked about this project with acquaintances, people's reactions were almost unanimous. They linked the Mohawks to the crisis of the '90s[4], violence, casinos, etc. However, the role of the Mohawk Traditional Council is to preserve the *Kanienke'ha'ka* language, to protect the tradition, and uphold the Two Row Wampum. Above all, the Council's duty is to protect and perpetuate the Great Law of Peace and Understanding in order to re-establish matrilineal authority back into Creation.

The Mohawk Traditional Council of Kahnawake has nothing to do with corruption, which is a result of *male dominance*. Since the term appears several times in the book, it is very important for the reader to understand that it does not refer to men necessarily, but rather to a human behaviour that has become widespread all around the planet. Today, many women manifest male dominance while many men are capable of great respect for womanhood. It is therefore necessary, when reading this book, to interpret the words male dominance as a lifestyle that is extremely harmful for life on

3. Political organization imposed under federal jurisdiction, in which members are elected.
4. In the summer of 1990, the Mohawk rallied to defend their land against an expansion project of a golf course. The Mohawk wanted to buy the land in question a year before the expansion project, but the government prevented this transaction. A year later, the developers of the golf course planned an expansion. Tragic events occurred during this crisis: the death's of a Sûreté du Québec police officer and of a Mohawk elder. This outcome generated a negative perception by the Quebec population with regard to the Mohawk cause. What was dubbed the "Oka Crisis" lasted 78 days.

Earth—and that's the reason why Stuart Myiow dedicates his whole heart to denounce it.

When I first went to visit the Mohawk Traditional Council of Kahnawake, I was a little uncomfortable whenever they answered the phone, because they always use speaker mode. I thought their conversations did not concern me, and I was wondering about their motivation in carrying out their phone calls so openly . . . until I realized that nothing is hidden with them; not only is speech sacred, but what is said is assumed so as well. Integrity, loyalty, truth, sharing, honesty, courage, respect are honoured at the Longhouse; that's why I feel good, I feel at home with the people of the Traditional Council. Their lifestyle satisfies me and lets my Eagle fly in complete freedom.

The writing was completed through a process that imposed itself on me. Without immediately understanding why, I went along with it. Indeed, when I began to write, I followed a work plan I had prepared almost a year earlier. But when I tried to produce the chapters according to that plan, I couldn't do it. Every time I wanted to work with a man, something happened that caused me to stop—the mysterious disappearance of memos in my dictaphone, for example. With women, things fell into place quickly and easily. So it is with them I was able to start. Along the way, I understood why.

According to Mohawk tradition, the Creation comes from a woman, Sky Woman. All life, in its early embryonic phase, begins as female, and then, if designated, turns male. When I realized that my writing efforts, in spite of myself, were in harmony with this natural order, I reorganized the work plan to remain faithful to the cycle of life. Thus, the first parts that I produced deal with the women. In this sense, the book followed the order already established with the first living being.

Because of my contact with the Native people, my concept of time has completely changed. Natives are not stressed nor rushed. They don't hurry anyone along, and I never observed any sign of impatience toward anyone concerning time. It's enough to drive crazy anyone who is used to stress and time constraints. For my part, I received this teaching as a relief. Since working with Native people, I have learned to let go: Let go of my control over others, let go of the need to control time, since everything, regardless, always ends up being perfect at the right moment. And therefore, I shed my stress . . .

Even if stress has less influence on me, it does not mean that I am not preoccupied. The current state of the planet worries me. The melting of the Poles, nuclear waste, razed forests, polluted water . . . but especially humanity's dawdling in the face of all those threats leads me to an obvious conclusion: Life in all its forms is endangered. We can no longer deny that our harmful actions— along with our inaction in ending this destruction—is leading to extremely serious consequences.

As a woman, I identify myself with our Mother Earth. Like her, and like any woman, it falls to me to transmit and preserve life. Despite my fears about the destructive wave breaking over the planet, I choose to focus on the tiny seed that I hold in my hand. And as much as it is humanly possible, I will keep it safe. I will protect it as long as I breathe, because even if the wave rages and destroys numerous lives, this seed carries the hope of life. To find the necessary strength for this role, I sink my roots deep into the belly of our Mother Earth, and I stand against this wave, defending the truth. Thus my true identity can be deployed, the one that gives me the power to preserve the seed of life.

THANK YOU

From the bottom of my heart, I thank every person who holds the speaking feather in this book. Their words came out of their soul to merge into an anthem of Creation and a rallying cry for the well-being of women, our Mother Earth and our Grandmother Moon.

Captain Paul Watson
Katsitenserio (Stuart Junior) Myiow
Tioronhiate (Stuart Senior) Myiow
Rorahkwaieshon Myiow
Kaneratentha Cross
Messinak Kassutasset
Aki Songideye Ikwe
Maniteu-Ishkueu
Tin Ifsen
Edith Mora Castelán
Raymond Stone Iwaasa
Yvan Bombardier
Brian Sarwer-Foner
Lucie Mainguy
Holly Dressel

Thank you, *nia:wen, migwetch, tshinashkumitin, tanemmirt, nayeche', go raibh maith agat, merci!*

GUYLAINE CLICHE

 Katsitenserio

Stuart Myiow Junior

Teio'rihwenton
Opening

First, as my mother taught me, the Mohawk man—or any man—is supposed to stand when facing women, or anyone else, when he speaks. He is not supposed to sit; otherwise people cannot decode his body language. If this man sits, he could lie. What my mother also taught me about *Kaianerahse'rakó:wa*, the Great Law of Peace and Understanding, is that I always have to identify myself. I am Katsitenserio, which means "Pretty bird". This is the name that my mother gave me. I also identify my mother by her name: Kahawenontie, which means "She carries the grapes".

When she was alive, she carried the sacred title of Female Chief into the *Kaianerahse'rakó:wa* in the Longhouse. My mother taught me that every man, before getting up and talking, must remember where he comes from. So I begin by thanking the first being of all Creation: *Ieronhiakaiehronon*, the Sky Woman. I thank her, but I do not settle for simply thanking her, I ask her to watch what I say, because when I speak, I stand before her. I ask her to listen to my words. I also ask her to help me and guide me, so that my words are not lies, but are the truth.

I also thank the beating heart of our Mother Earth: our Grandmother Moon, whom we all know, especially women, since the Moon visits them thirteen times a year and unites women with Mother Earth and Grandmother Moon—all forming one.[5] Grandmother Moon moves the blood of life, not only in our bodies, but also in the body of our Mother Earth. Grandmother Moon is the beating heart of Mother Earth, the same way that we have a heart that beats in our own bodies. The function of our physical heart is exactly the same as the heart of Mother Earth.

Also, I thank our Mother Earth, because she is mother of us all; she is the mother of all that exists. We all come from the Earth, so we have to thank her. And as I mentioned about Sky Woman, whom I ask to guide my words, I also ask Grandmother Moon and Mother Earth to be with me and to watch my words. Thus, no bad word, or lie can be expressed.

---

5. In many Aboriginal nations, the menstrual period of the woman is called "Moon time."

Now, I thank all women, from the newest born baby girl to the eldest grandmother, since they are all mothers of our nations. If you carry a little girl in your womb right now, she has perhaps not yet arrived in this world and perhaps she has not given birth, but she is a woman, which makes her the mother of our nation. She must therefore be treated with great respect.

Whether they come from the other side of the world, are white, black or yellow: All women are our mothers—and even the youngest girls are our mothers and should be treated as such. This means that abuse against women must not be tolerated. Besides, we should not witness what we see in today's world. This is unacceptable.

Also, I want to thank all our ancestors who came before us and who carry the Good Mind. This does not exclude the fact that we all have ancestors who were stupid, who did bad things in this world, but we do not condemn them. In evolution, we reject what is bad and we build upon only what is good. So when we speak and we evolve, we identify what is bad and we know that we have nothing to do with it. We, therefore, ask our ancestors who bear wisdom to help us return to *Atonhetsera*, Spirit/True Power, and the real power of women: not the power that you want as women, but the real one.

There are men who covet the power, but it is not the real power of man. Some men are wrong. Some women also may go astray from the right path, even if they are women. We therefore ask our ancestors to help us bring the real power of *Atonhetsera*, the *Tekenitehio hate*, the Two Row Wampum, and the True Spirit of *Asen nikatarake* from the three Universal Clans: Turtle, Wolf and Bear, which are those of the *Kanienke'ha'ka*, the People of the Flint.

Let's specify that Mohawk means nothing. *Kanienke'ha'ka* really means something; same as Anishnabe means something, while the name one has given them, Algonquin, means absolutely nothing.

Moreover, when the Anishnabes speak, we identify with them while when the Mohawks speak, we are all *Kanienke'ha'ka*. However, this does not mean that the Anishnabes become Mohawks by blood relationship. Therefore, when we say that all are *Kanienke'ha'ka* when we are speaking, this does not mean that the Anishnabe, or people of any other nation, are considered *Kanienke'ha'ka*. This means I have to treat you like I would treat my brother or sister. Not only as a brother or a sister of another community, but within my family, because we all identify ourselves as being from the three Universal Clans no matter what nation we may be from.

Whether we are female or male, we are made of one and the other Universal Clan. We can never completely separate them from one another. However, if I was up against the wall and I had to identify my link to the Creator, I would be forced to say that it is feminine. Sky Woman began a song, and then she started to dance to the song of Creation. She showed us the way. So I follow her and I communicate with her.

This is how I identify myself because that's what my mother taught me. I follow her path into the Great Law of Peace and in ceremonies. I also identify myself as a son of our nations' mothers and of Sky Woman who is crying for the atonement of any injustice, oppression, all rapes, murders and wars inflicted upon the mothers all around the world. This requires that the imbalance of male dominance is stopped in order for our mothers to recover their natural authority. These women have the authority to report all crimes and trauma inflicted upon them by the male self-glorification process of of creating God in man's image which oppresses mothers by a false authority that man has given himself.

He carries the songs of his mother.

Sá'iontenekwenhsah'sats'te:ne
New Moon

Traditional Teachings

Welcome to the Longhouse,
where decisions are made in council,
where people live as one family,
where children grow up under the benevolent gaze of the elders,
where women are the authority.

Tioronhiate

Grandfather Stuart Myiow

Kasotshesera
The Elder

When I was born, I was given a name and I did not need to receive another name. My Mohawk name is Tioronhiate, which means "Bright Sky." I am from the Bear Clan, the elder of the Mohawk Traditional Council of Kahnawake, and the father of four sons of which Katsitenserio is the youngest. One day, one of my friends came to me because he wanted my help to catch three bears. Being from the Bear Clan, I accepted without any hesitation. To thank me, my friend gave me one. At one point, some kids scared the bear I was given. Frightened, the bear began to run and he broke his chain. At that time, we had a fence around the house; I ran after the bear which was about to go under that fence. At the moment I was to jump on his back and grab his hair, he turned around, then I jumped on him, between his front legs, I stood on him and I caught his mouth with both hands, so he would not bite me. My brother was on the other side of the fence and I shouted to him to put a rope around the bear's neck. Scared, he said "No way!" but even so, he brought me a rope that I put on the animal's nose to keep his mouth shut, then I wrapped it around his neck and I brought the bear back to where he was. After that event, because I did not have the proper equipment to keep the bear, the police took and drove him to some zoo. I never heard about him since.

In the opening, we gave our thanks to the creator, Sky Woman, then we did the same to Grandmother Moon, Mother Earth, and coming up to all the animals, the trees, the medicine, the water, the wind, the birds, and all that is around, reaching every life here and out into space. We are thankful, because anything that exists in nature gives us life. But right now, life is disappearing, so we have to remember where this life comes from. I am glad to speak throughout this book, which I hope is going to help fix what has been broken.

Teio'wenon'nia:nion
The Circles

In the past, things were different. People from different nations met and formed circles in which they exchanged ideas. If someone had a particular problem regardless of the type of problem (children, elders and so on), others shared their knowledge on the subject: "We will talk about such a problem, because you know something about it." This is how we helped each other. There was always someone who knew which medicine was needed. We exchanged while sitting and talking. This is how we maintained peace between our nations.

Onkwehonwe Takaion
People From the Past

I don't know which way you live out your spirituality, in a traditional way or some other way, but know that when you will leave this world, it is not finished. It could happen that people who have left appear to you, but it occurs only when they have a good reason.

Here is a little example: One day, I was on the phone with a friend from Akwesasne. During the conversation, I was watching through the window and I said to one of my sons to go check what this woman wanted at that time, my son Stuart was swimming in the quarry across the road in front of our house. He had a truck that was parked on the edge, on the rocks, and was walking by the edge of the rock in front of the truck. Suddenly, he fell many meters straight down onto jagged rocks. He only hurt his feet, but could have been killed. This is when I saw that woman crossing the road during my phone call. So when my other son, whom I asked to check what this woman wanted, went to meet her, she had disappeared.

This is just a small part of the experiences you could have when you are in harmony with nature. So now you know that people of the past can come back if they really have to. Whenever a person of that kind disappears in front of your eyes, it is for a reason that you have to find out. One thing is certain, it will make you think about life.

Atetshenserá
The Dreams

All dreams are important. If you have a dream, that is good. You have the same dream, it is better. If you do it a third time, then you move. The only way to understand a dream is by talking with other people about it. We have to get their insights to understand what the dream means. Once the dream is understood, then the person can be told what needs to be done or what type of ceremony is necessary. But today, not all of my people think in this way. They have been brainwashed by religion, which is the worst thing that has existed on the face of our Mother Earth.

There is so much more that has to be said, nevertheless I can see that tomorrow we will draw closer and we won't have any reason to be mad at each other, but today we must learn how to live together while respecting our identities.

 Katsitenserio

Stuart Myiow Junior

Kanosesne
The Longhouse

Within the *Kanienke'ha'ka* Nation, the roles of women and men are clearly established, allowing the people fulfilling these roles to live in balance, peace and harmony. All *Kanienke'ha'ka* women are considered to be the greatest gift in Creation as "Mothers of the Nation." By Law, the *Kanienke'ha'ka* are a matrilineal society; therefore, as life begins from our mothers, so do all actions and decisions. The men of the nation have the honour and duty of ensuring that matrilineal authority is respected, protected and upheld on all levels. True matrilineal authority is achieved through the balancing of female and male powers. In this regard, we must understand that the word "matrilineal" does not mean the same as "matriarchal". Often people who are not familiar with *Kanienke'ha'ka* culture confuse the two. Matrilineal means that women have power without domination, in balance with men. The matriarchal and patriarchal words both carry a domination meaning.

In a family, an expectant father must go through the pregnancy along with the mother to ensure that he also develops a bond with the child and that his mind is prepared for fatherhood by living through and understanding the life-bearing process. He must also comfort and aid the expectant mother in any fashion necessary. It is the responsibility of the father to ensure the mother is not exposed to any anger or aggression at any time, but especially during pregnancy.

Moreover, it is the responsibility of the women to ensure the physical and mental well-being of all pregnant women. The first hands that touch a child at birth must be the loving hands of the grandmother, if possible. Child-birthing is women's business; therefore, women exclusively deliver the children. However, in certain situations, a man may be asked for assistance: for example, if a woman goes into labour in a location where there is no woman present to help her deliver. Female relatives of the mother-to-be (blood relatives or clan family) might also assist in child-birthing. They must also ensure adequate care of the afterbirth, in burying it close to the Longhouse so that the children will always return home and know their place in the physical world.

At birth, the children inherit their birthright (clan) from the mother. Children are welcomed into the world by the grandmother and relatives within the clan. The father of the child and his clan family will then welcome the child. Although children carry the identity of the clan family of their mother, children are gifts to the Longhouse and the people collectively celebrate every new life.

Before a child is given a name, the choice is discussed with the elder women of the clan family of the mother. The female chiefs (clan-mothers) also are consulted to ensure that the name is available and appropriate for the child. The mother, father or a member of the Longhouse may have dreams or visions in regards to an expectant child, which they will share with the people and which may influence name selection. The child is officially named at the next *Atonwa* Ceremony by the female and male chiefs of that clan family. Women must be grounded (feet planted) in their territory. This is important for the stability of the children because our identity is directly tied to the Earth. Women mostly stay within their territory, with their clan families, as women are the foundation of the clans and the Longhouse.

After a child is born and named, she or he has left the spirit realm within the womb of their mother and takes their place upon Mother Earth. All children belong to the women. During the early years of childhood, a child is regarded as still being so close to the mother that they are still nearly one body, as the mother breastfeeds her child. Breast milk is considered the mother's lifeblood.

Mothers speak on behalf of their children and represent them in councils or ceremonies, unless they delegate that power to the father or someone else. Ensuring that children have positive role models in their fathers and uncles is instrumental in raising healthy well-balanced children. The entire clan family raises the children together. It would not be unusual, traditionally, for children to be breastfed by different women. This loving and supportive atmosphere is instrumental in maintaining a life of happiness and stability based on the Great Law of Peace. It also allows those who don't have children to experience the happiness and fulfillment of motherhood or fatherhood. In doing so, it guarantees, through the collective, the physical, mental and spiritual well-being of every person by ensuring that everyone is a mother and father of the nation.

A child grows up in constant contact with the mother and female relatives within the clan family. In the first year of life, babies are kept in a cradleboard made of wood and sinew. The child's mother will keep her child tied to her back as she gardens or does chores. The cradleboard not only keeps a fragile infant safe but also plays an instrumental role in the nurturing of the child, aiding in the development of a firm and steadfast mind.

Traditionally, children are given a corn-husk doll to play with. From birth, children mimic their mothers and learn from them—especially the daughters who are the future mothers of the nation. The fathers and uncles of the clan play an instrumental role in the child's life, playfully teasing or wrestling with the children and teaching them life skills. As boys grow older, their father and uncles within the clan play a bigger role as they are role models. It is essential that the adult men teach young boys about respecting and protecting all female things in Creation. Within this family structure, it is impossible for a man to violate or trespass upon any female, regardless of age, in any way whatsoever.

Children growing up in the Longhouse are observed by the women who help them discern their character and potential role within the Longhouse. The best qualities, the strengths in the children, are identified and encouraged by the women. All children will be guided and nurtured to develop into future chiefs of the nation, as female or male leaders (clan mothers and chiefs). It is the duty of the women to select individuals for Chieftainship Titles. The women must also watch the people carefully to correct any wrongs and to ensure that the Great Law of Peace is adhered to. The men also carry out this role under the women's (particularly the female chiefs) watchful eye.

As children reach the age of adolescence, they are monitored for the first signs of adulthood. The people must ensure that adolescents have been adequately taught all the necessary skills and traits for marriage, parenting and the strengthening of a healthy human collective.

Once their first moon (menstrual period) begins, females are helped, taught and guided into womanhood. Many of these teachings are done through Moon Ceremonies, where women are taught the essence of femininity and female power (body and spirit). After the path to womanhood has begun, the girl child is thanked for the beautiful role she has filled with the people and then she takes her place as a woman of the Longhouse.

Boys spend more time with their father and uncles learning the skills of men. Their transition into manhood is also fostered by the men during men's meetings or Moon Ceremonies. It is essential that all young boys who are beginning on their paths to manhood are taught and shown how to carry out the ceremonies, how to honour the female in this world and how to maintain the balance between female and male powers to ensure a healthy evolution.

The Longhouse and garden are managed by the women, as those domains belong to them. Women defer to men if they need a tool or a cradleboard to be made, or if they need something else constructed for them. The majority of a man's time is spent on the structural upkeep of the various shelters and Longhouse grounds. The men must do most of the physical work, particularly things that may be harmful for a woman to do. Men share responsibilities in most of the tasks carried out by the women but with utmost respect for the women's roles as the leaders of the nation. Women have more tasks centered on the home and gardens where they spend the majority of their time with the children.

Men's tasks and responsibilities tend to keep them away from the home or even the territory for various periods of time. It is the responsibility of the men to keep the territory clear of any obstruction that may harm the people. These tasks are done in simple ways, such as clearing paths of sharp stones or removing branches at eye level so the women do not have to worry for the children's safety, and/or more complexly, removing aggressive physical threats by chasing away predatory animals. They also constantly monitor the land for any foreign or domestic threats.

The people of the Longhouse live closely with Mother Earth. The women determine the time to plant and provide the seeds that they are responsible for gathering and storing. The main sustenance of the *Kanienke'ha'ka* has always been the Three Sisters: Corn, Bean and Squash. This traditional diet is supplemented by other planted vegetables and natural foods. Medicines[6] are also cultivated.

The women must be aware of the weather and state of the gardens in order to determine when the earth should be turned over. Men help to prepare the soil for planting. By Law, they must work their hands into the earth to prepare the soil for the planting of the Three Sisters. Women are responsible for planting the seeds in the garden, followed by the men who will water them. The women are responsible for storing the harvested foods and to ensure that there is enough food to sustain life for the winter months. Hunting and fishing is done during all seasons but always in balance with Creation, so as not to deplete the resources.

As adolescents mature into adults, the time for courtship and marriage approaches. Young girls and boys are taught to respect themselves and their bodies and to hold the latter sacred. Marriage in the *Kanienke'ha'ka* way of life is different than in other societies. After a woman and man of different clans express their desire to be together, marriage is a highly personal ceremony. The woman and the man pledge to each other but mainly to the people of the Longhouse, to be good examples, to live together within the Great Law of Peace, to be a rafter added to the house, to protect and to parent all the children within the nation.

Marriage within the Longhouse is a commitment from two individuals to the people to uphold the Law as one. The vows, the words, and the gifts exchanged are decided on by the woman and man. The clan family of the man provides a meal for the guests.

Ideally, when they marry, women must not be taken from their territory or clan family. If a woman chooses a man from another nation, he would relocate to live with his wife and raise their children in her territory with her clan family unless conditions provide

---

6. See note 1, page 18. In this case, it is a matter of medicinal plants.

for an alternative arrangement. This is not to mean that a woman cannot travel to and relocate in another territory if she so desires, but she is generally linked with her community and people. If the married couple lives together, it is in the Longhouse belonging to the woman, but the man must still sit with his clan for meetings and councils, as well as perform tasks for his mother and clan family.

Couples do not necessarily have to marry in order to experience life together or to have children. They are also not obligated to stay together as it would be detrimental to show children the chaos that ensues when a woman and man stay together if they are out of balance with each other. Any person within the Longhouse may offer words of encouragement or state openly when they see that either person within a marriage is conducting themselves out of balance or disrespectfully toward the other. The people may remind the couple of their commitments when necessary until their days are done within the garden of life.

Ceremonies are based on the natural cycles of Creation, most of which are marked by stages of growth and changes in nature as well as gardens, the moons, temperature, frost, rain, and so on. Ceremonies are never planned by a set time except for that of Mid-Winter. There are 13 Full Moon Ceremonies and 13 New Moon Ceremonies, which identify the 13 Moon cycles. This is an instrumental part of *Kanienke'ha'ka* life and a major source of the women's power. This is why the women must have their hands and feet in the soil, so as not to break their connection with our Mother Earth, allowing them to always be connected to the complete energy flow from Sky Woman to Grandmother Moon to our Mother Earth, through the women, interpreted by the men, and then finally back to the Earth. The people must watch the signs in the garden to identify the changes in the cycles of Creation.

The women must be present at all councils and ceremonies to ensure that everything is carried out according to the Great Law of Peace, and to keep the men on track. No council is legally open unless the Female Chief or an appointed representative is present. And no council is closed legally unless first granted by the women.

Women also have several tasks during the ceremonies, such as teaching the people, watching and caring for the children, cleaning and preparing the Longhouse or garden, providing food, preparing medicines, and so on.

Men, for their part, stand ready and present themselves to councils on the requests and directions given by the women. They also prepare for the ceremonies in any way that is necessary, and they keep a watchful eye on the children, especially the young boys, to ensure that they are respectful of the women and the ceremonies. Finally, throughout the entirety of every council, the female chiefs (clan mothers) sit side by side with the male chiefs and direct them when necessary, except in men's or war councils.

Obviously, the roles of everyone within the Longhouse are well defined and when each one does what he or she is supposed to do, peace reigns over the *Kanienke'ha'ka*'s life.

Katsitenserio
Stuart Myiow Junior

Asen Nikatarake
The three Universal Clans

Several nations have their own clans, many clans. In the five nations, the Onontake have 13 clans, which is very numerous. We even have a clan called "Potato Clan" and one called "Opposite side of the hand". Moreover, this clan is the one that facilitates the understanding of both sides of a situation. These names have deep meanings, but if you see someone on the street and say to him: "Hey! This person is from the Opposite-side-of-the hand Clan.", almost nobody will understand what it means, but our people know.

The Turtle, Wolf and Bear Clans are universal, not only for all nations here on Turtle Island[7], but they are universal around the Earth. They are everywhere, Turtle, Wolf and Bear, in one form or another. Turtles are found both in water and on land. This is why the Turtle Clan is the one who owns the Longhouse, which it carries it on its back. The people of this clan are recognized as the oldest fibre of Creation, since DNA life itself begins with the Turtle, thereby conferring upon it authority. We also have in the rest of the world similarities with the Wolf Clan or the Bear Clan. For example, in Australia, there are the dingoes, which are not exactly

---

7. Part of the world that includes North and South America.

wolves but are similar and play the same role. Same for the bear: If we go to the North, we have polar bears, or pandas in China, and so on.

The Three Universal Clans are intrinsic to our Mother Earth. However, they are not what you think they are when you look at the surface. They are not turtles, wolves or bears. That's what they represent within Creation. What they represent is found at a very small scale, at a molecular level of Creation, in smaller molecules assembled together to generate every creature. It is in these molecules that you will find the Turtle, Wolf and Bear Clans. This is the foundation of each particle of Creation and we have always known it. This is what scientists call protons, neutrons and electrons, even if these words don't carry any meaning allowing for human comprehension. This is where you will find the Turtle, the Wolf and the Bear. This is inherent in all living things at all levels: from the smallest to the largest including collective consciousness where we are. All people carry within them these identities. Even in the nail of my big toe, the molecules therein are composed of protons, neutrons and electrons: Turtle, Wolf and Bear. They are not only found in the nail of my toe, but in every part of my being.

Today, scientists—who, let's not forget, are not native—discovered these molecules, but they cannot make sense of them; they refer to them with words that have no meaning. The way they identify them does not connect these molecules to us as members of our family. They are studying the phenomenon and, like everything else, it is just an observation. Look what they observed when they came to what they called the New World. What did they say? A complete inversion of the truth. They don't know what they observe. They have to be told, they have to be taught. We're the ones who have to remind them of all these things: how society is made, its structure and order that is in every fibre it is composed of.

When we enter the Longhouse, when we enter a circle, like any *Kanienke'ha'ka* we advance and know immediately where we should sit. I know who I am, so I know where I have to sit and I

48

know that my brothers and sisters of the Wolf Clan must sit with me with our backs turned to the north, while the Bear Clan will sit with their backs to the south, and men of the Turtle Clan will sit with backs to the east and women to the west. Thus, they can keep an eye on everything that takes place within the house.

Because men are separated from women in the Turtle Clan, one could say, "Oh? Why are men and women separated? Are we not all equal?" Well no, we are not equal. I'll never be the equal of a woman. Never. I cannot present myself before my mother saying that I am her equal. I would be very pretentious to tell my mother that I am her equal. How could I tell women I am their equal? How could any man claim to be their equal? Women have brought children into this world. What man has done this? What man has given birth and brought children into this world? There is no man who will be the equal to a woman, even to the youngest female baby in this world.

Nevertheless, the role of men is important. But according to the Great Law of Peace and Understanding, we know our place. When we need to reconnect to our roots, we return to Sky Woman. I know I can do it. Once I get there, I find that the first being is female. So how could I be equal to a woman? It is impossible. She created me. That is why we have never understood how, on the other side of the great ocean, the man is able to oppress, rape and kill his mother. How can he make war for generations? It's suicidal behaviour.

In another vein, the word *okwaho* means "wolf". This clan is *Ronataion:ni*, which means "Those who lead the way". It is the role of the Wolf Clan to take initiatives the Bear Clan deliberates and the Turtle Clan approves. Of course, one might ask why the Bear Clan sits south, why the Wolves sit north. Why would it not be the Bears who would sit north? Well, bears hibernate during the cold weather. They hibernate because they come from the south. The bear is not made to withstand the cold during winter. The wolf stands out at any temperature day or night. All the time. He is always out, cleaning Creation. That is his role. This is why, in humans, we differentiate those who follow the path from those who lead the way: *Ronataion:ni*. This is exactly what the wolves do in Creation: they run, and they decide which lineages will remain. For example, there are many rabbits, certainly, but there are also many wolves. Wolves could therefore decide to remove the rabbits. This is how they lead the way in which all things in Creation are subject. They initiate the DNA strands of the planet that are woven by the Earth's magnetic field. These are unimaginably sacred roles within Creation that true beings must return to.

Ratiniaton
The Turtle Clan

The turtle has 13 squares on its shell representing the 13 Cycles of Ceremonies. Turtle shells are used to make rattles used in ceremonies, specifically to perform the *Astowakowa, The Great Feather Dance* (Creator's Dance). *Ratiniaton* represents the Owners of the House and the Fire Keepers of the Mohawk Nation. Men of the Turtle Clan sit with their backs to the east (where the Sun rises) and women to the west. The Turtle is honoured as being the Owner of the House, as they are one of the oldest living things, dating back to the Creation story. The Great Turtle carries our Mother Earth upon its back. Within the Mohawk Council, the Turtle Clan members are the verifiers. All business of the House is presented to them for final consideration. The three Turtle Clan Chieftainship Titles are: *Tekarihoken, Aionwatha* and *Satekariwateh*. In addition to the three Chieftainship Titles, the Turtle Clan also holds the Title of War Chief for the Mohawk Nation. (There is only one War Chief for the Nation.)

Turtle Clan people are very consistent and determined. They prefer a calm atmosphere and are disturbed by confrontation. They are generally neutral in most situations. Sometimes, like the turtle, they hide in their shell until things have calmed down. They can be stubborn at times and do not adjust to change very quickly. Most Turtle Clan people are thought of as shy because they are not as outspoken or opinionated as people from the other two clans. They also take more time to let go of anger or irritation because they would prefer not to be faced with a confrontation.

Turtle Clan people take their time to think before they respond to a question or solve an issue. Because they are neutral, they are good at mediating to solve disputes. Like the turtle, they have a very strong protective shell and it may take time to get to know them. As a collective, Turtles are wise and fair.

Ronataion:ni
The Wolf Clan

Ronataion:ni are "Those Who Lead the Way". The Wolf Clan sits with their backs to the north (where the cold winds come from). The Wolf Clan is known as the "Well" in which all issues and manners of business are dropped into and managed on behalf of the Longhouse. As the "Well", the Wolf Clan are the Initiators of business during the counselling process (the Bear Clan are the Deliberators, the Turtle Clan are the Verifiers). The Wolf Clan representatives determine the order of business based upon the collective knowledge of the Great Law of Peace, explaining what issues are presented on the council floor to be decided by the people. It is the role of the Wolf Clan to ensure that the Council stays on topic and that order is maintained. The three Wolf Clan Chieftainship Titles are: *Sarenho:wane, Teionhehkwen* and *Orenhre'ko:wa*. In addition to these three titles, the Wolf Clan takes on the role of the "Well" in the Grand Council of the Five Nations Confederacy.

Wolf Clan people, like the wolf, are very intelligent and cunning. Their strength is in their knowledge of the Great Law of Peace of which they must have expertise in order to properly facilitate Longhouse business. They are great thinkers and doers. They are generally outspoken and opinionated. They love to debate and deliberate on issues and can pursue issues aggressively at times. They can also be very diplomatic, particularly when handling business, while staying calm and focused. Wolf Clan people do not let their emotions hinder their thoughts; they keep a cool demeanour under pressure. They are also great orators and can respond to issues quickly without requiring much time.

As a family, the Wolf Clan is a group of very independent and capable people. They have a candid and forthright nature which may give the appearance of aggressiveness when they interact with the others. However, they are fiercely loyal to each other and will instantly bind together to defend a member of the clan family. They are very playful and loving with their children but will push and test each other often. Wolf Clan members are very capable as individuals but their strength lies in being a group. The Wolf Clan is the mechanism within society that constantly pushes its collective human evolution into every aspect of life

Rotihskare:wake
The Bear Clan

Rotihskare:wake are the deliberators of the three counselling clans. They sit with their backs to the south, where the warm winds come from. Due to their medicine[8], they are able to detect any problems with great prudence within the application process on any given issue. The three Bear Clan Chieftainship Titles are: *Tehana'Karin:ne, Ahstawenserenhtha* and *Shoskoharo:wane.*

The Bear Clan has the highest number of people of all three Mohawk clans due to the fact that visitors, or those who do not carry the birthright of one of the clans, automatically fall under the "protection" of the Bear Clan. This clan acts as a surrogate family to the visitor for the duration of their interaction with the Longhouse until the visitor departs or their request for adoption into a clan is accepted. The Bear Clan will ensure that all people who fall under their protection are well cared for and mentored on Longhouse matters and the Great Law of Peace. This policy also protects the Longhouse people and Great Law of Peace from being

---

8. See note 1, page 18.

hindered or altered by the "Bad Mind" or from interference from those who may not know our ways.

Bear Clan people have a very strong physical power coupled with a very strong reactionary nature, which makes for a sometimes seemingly abrasive and aggressive personality. However, their unyielding side and often ferocious power is tempered by the gentleness of the female, disciplining them emotionally. By nature they are capable of taking mockery, teasing and abuse. However, when they have reached a point where their patience has run thin, like an awakened hibernating bear, they can be very fierce. Although they never forget a negative situation, they are always more than willing to move past it to a more positive outcome for everyone.

The Bear Clan people enjoy helping others and are good listeners. They flourish in a relaxed environment. Leisure is a strong part of their lives; however, they are always willing to help with any problem or ailment, whether physical, emotional, or spiritual. Due in large part to their nature, Bear Clan people have the function of retaining knowledge of the Sacred Medicine. As a group, the Bear Clan has great healing power due to their acute knowledge of the energy transfer between all living things on our Mother Earth.

 Katsitenserio
Stuart Myiow Junior

Kaianerahsera'ko:wa Ne Skennen
The Great Law of Peace and Understanding

In the Longhouse, all the facts must be known by all. All truths must be known, which means that all truths must be put on the table. If you know the truth and I do not know it, you have to put it on the table for me, if not, then corruption is promoted.

(GREAT LAW OF PEACE AND UNDERSTANDING)

I n the north-eastern woodlands of Turtle Island, there was once a family of people quite simply known as the *Onkwehón:we* (the True Beings). These people were bound together as one by four sacred ceremonies, which are the four stages of Creation that all life is based upon, keeping the balance between women and men.

Thousands of years ago, this family divided into five factions. These factions eventually became five individual nations, which are known as the: Mohawk (*Kanienka'ha'ka*), Oneida, Onondaga, Cayuga, and Seneca. These divisions grew into war, destroying the balance between women and men, and devolving us into a male-dominated society. This war progressed to such an extent that we exposed ourselves to ruin.

Tekanawita (the Peace Maker) then came to the people of the Five Nations and united them under the *Kaianerahsere'kó:wa ne skennen*, the Great Law of Peace and Understanding, establishing the Five Nations Confederacy. This enabled the men to return out of the darkness of war and evolve back up to the level of the women, restoring their balance with them, but this time establishing matrilineal authority as Law. This Law returned us to the natural design of a matrilineal society, making the people and the land flourish for over 1500 years, until the people from the other side of the world (Europeans) came here to destroy the Great Peace.

From 1492, for over 350 years (late 1800s), the foreign influence of war, disease, hate-driven religions, brainwashing education and male-dominated society divided the Confederacy and destroyed the Great Law to the point where the Chiefs saw it necessary to write this Law down in order to preserve it for future generations.

Here in Kahnawake, through the late 1930s to the mid 1940s, a written version of the Law existed in the form of a "black book." This version eventually disappeared while in the possession of one of our families.

In 1946, the Confederacy was in resurgence. Over the next 20 years, the Great Law of Peace and Understanding was re-emerging and being applied. People were becoming familiar with the Law, and the Longhouse was becoming strong once again. For almost 30 years, people were living in peace. But in 1973, some issues between the Chiefs and the Band Council[9] (a British genocidal construct first created in 1850s) caused a major division within the House, creating the illegal[10] organization of the Warrior Society[11]. This is the exact point in time when people—mostly influenced by

9. See note 4, page 22.
10. In the passages of this book that speak of "illegality" or "legality", these words do not refer to the government's justice, but to the Law of Peace of *Kanienke'ha'ka*.
11. Mohawk organization created in the '70s, whose activities are controversial.

those who did not carry the birthright within the Warrior Society and the elected Band Council system—became disrespectful to the authority of Women and Men Chiefs. What emerged from this poison injected into our community was a way of thinking opposite to Law: anarchy.

Since then, money gained through businesses conducted outside the Great Law of Peace (cigarettes, alcohol and so on) became the new authority. This is when the people of Kahnawake embarked upon the path of *democrapitalism*, of greed and division, which they consciously spread throughout the rest of the Confederacy. At this point, it drove the entire Confederacy to its utter ruin and handed over all the faces who are yet beneath the Earth (future generations) to the destructive force of *democrapitalism*.

The worst illness infecting our Mother Earth is democrapitalism, which is the evolution of colonialism. Today, almost 7 billion people are governed by the laws of capitalism and are controlled by democracy. Human beings who have succumbed to colonialism think that they are the most advanced society ever and that democracy is the pinnacle of human existence, but it is actually the bottom of human existence. Through democracy, people have the notion that, because they vote, they can electively decide. But actually, democracy enslaves people and lets them believe that, by voting, they participate in a process that empowers them. In reality, it takes the power away from them, because democracy is controlled by capitalism and the captains of industry; the modern version of early European pirates.

Colonialism is still advancing around the world, but on a different level. As a result of colonialism, we have received a false education; we have been taught a man-made religion and that killing our Mother Earth is the way to live. Killing Mother Earth is no way to live because in killing the Earth, we are killing the environment in which we live and we are leaving humanity with no way to sustain itself. So this is the way that *democrapitalism* represents the improved version of colonialism, and this is definitely the opposite of the Laws of Creation.

So, over the years following the 1973 events, the Longhouse was very unstable. The division caused much infighting and espionage. This hindered all functions in the House and spread like wildfire throughout the entire Confederacy, duplicating the exact same division in each territory, which erupted and caused Mohawk blood to spill onto the floor of the Grand Council in Onantake in 1974.

In the fall of 1977, some people—including a woman—attacked my brother and another man on Longhouse grounds. In the early 1980s the Warrior Society started the cigarette trade, and by the mid 1980s, many high school kids were dropping out of school to join the Warrior Society, getting paid $300 per week to drive around protecting their cigarette stores with AK-47 rifles in their hands.

In the early spring of 1988, things were heating up so much over the cigarette industry, and everything else we were opposed to, that our home got shot up; sprayed with machine gun fire by cowards under the cover of darkness at 5 a.m.—just missing my mother. Ballistics was called in but no investigation took place by the Peacekeepers[12] for they knew where the weapons came from and where that trail would lead: the Warrior Society and their creator, the elected mayor of the band council, who also controlled the Peacekeepers.

Afterwards, early in the following winter during a snowstorm, someone attempted to burn down our new Longhouse. Footprints could be followed in the snow, but once again the Peacekeepers didn't investigate. These acts of terrorism caused some people to live in fear within our Longhouse, creating a division between those who just wanted to carry out the ceremonies in peace, and those of us who wanted the Law to be carried out.

If anyone is ashamed of something they have done in the past, it would only be because it was wrong. But from the moment these questions become matters of national importance, then the wrong they are ashamed of is detrimental to all future generations and must be corrected. We have a larger responsibility beyond just our

---

12. Local police on the Kahnawake reserve, under the jurisdiction of the provincial and federal governments.

own people. We have a responsibility to protect and defend our Mother Earth. The entire world is waging an economic war on her and we, of the Five Nations Confederacy, have the medicine that could stop the destruction that is being inflicted upon her: the Great Law of Peace and Understanding.

During nine meetings we, from the Traditional Mohawk Council of Kahnawake, made the effort to reconstitute the Law. We have finalized a version, which is the most complete written version to date. Of course it is not the Law itself in its entirety; it is a reference from which to start.

The only way to learn this Law in its entirety is to experience the living breathing process of the oral tradition in an officially sanctioned Recital. The shortest Recital that I have personally participated in was at the late Ann Jock's place in the Mohawk Territory of Akwesasne in 1987—which, due to time restraints, took only five days. The longest Recital that has taken place in probably over the last 150 years, which I have personally participated in, was at the Longhouse Up-The-Hill here in the Mohawk Territory of Kahnawake, which took a total of 26 days. We must also make it clear that only one who is within the Circle of the Great Peace can conduct a Recital, for the Great Law of Peace is a living breathing entity that lives only where it is upheld and exercised.

Due to the fact that there are formidable forces that want to destroy this Law by manipulating its contents to suit their own needs, we find it necessary to protect the validity of this document by limiting its distribution to just officially sanctioned copies that are signed by the Mohawk Traditional Council here in Kahnawake and stamped with the official seal of the Five Nations Confederacy. If you have a document that is not signed and sealed in this way, it is not a sanctioned copy and is thus invalid.

The Great Law of Peace and Understanding has more than 100 wampums[13] divided into about 20 groups. For the purposes of

---

13. Wampum (an abbreviation of *wampumpeague*, an Algonquin word): beaded belt carrying an official message. In the Great Law of Peace, each item of the Act is defined by a wampum.

this chapter, I will therefore limit myself to quote the section titles alone, and I will share a summary of wampum 1 and 2.

So, here are the titles of the sections:

1- I am Tekanawita
2- Duties and Functions of the Central Fire, Onontake Nation
3- Structure and Rules Governing the International Grand Council
4- Rights, Duties and Qualifications of Chiefs
5- Rights of the People in Relation to Chieftainship Titles
6- Installation of Pine Tree Chiefs
7- Names, Duties and Rights of Big Knives
8- Messengers and Runners
9- Clans and Consanguinity
10- Official Symbolism
11- Laws of Adoption
12- Laws of Immigration
13- Rights of Foreign Nations
14- Rights and Powers of Waging Peace
15- Treason or Secession of a Nation
16- Rights of the People of the Five Nations
17- Rights and Ceremonies Protected
18- The Installation Song
19- Protection of the House
20- Funeral Address

Here are now the wampums 1 and 2 that constitute the *I am Tekanawita* section:

1- I AM TEKANAWITA, UNDER THE AUTHORITY OF THE WOMEN HEIRS, CLAN MOTHERS, SACRED TITLEHOLDERS OF THE LAND, ALONG WITH THE UNITED CHIEFS OF THE FIVE NATIONS CONFEDERACY I plant the Great Tree of

Peace. I plant it in your territory, ATOTARHO, and the Onontake Nation, in the territory of you who are the FIREKEEPERS.

I name the tree TIONERATASEKOWA—Great White Pine. Under the shade of this Great Tree of Peace we spread the soft white feathery down of the globe thistle as seats for you, ATOTARHO, and your cousin Chiefs.

We place you upon those seats, there beneath the shade of the spreading branches of the Great Tree of Peace. There shall you sit and watch the Council Fire of the Five Nations Confederacy, and all the affairs of the Five Nations shall be transacted at this place before you, ATOTARHO and your cousin Chiefs, by the united Chiefs of the Five Nations Confederacy.

2- Roots have spread out from the Tree of the Great Peace, one to where the Sun rises, one to where the Sun sets, one to where the cold winds come from and one to where the warm summer rains come from. The names of these roots are The Great White Roots and their nature is Peace and Strength.

If any person, or nation, outside of the Five Nations wishes to abide by the Laws of the Great Peace and make known their disposition to the Chiefs of the Confederacy, they may trace the roots to the base of the tree. If their minds are clean and promise to abide by the Laws of the Great Council of Peace, they shall be welcomed to take shelter beneath the tree, TIONERATASEKOWA.

The great Creator has placed atop the Great Tree of Peace the mighty Akweks (Eagle), the messenger of the Creator, who is able to see afar. If the mighty Eagle sees in the distance any evil approaching or any danger threatening, the messenger will at once warn the united people of the Confederacy.

Ton'taionkhiion nahoten iohton:on
The Return of What Was Lost

Re-establishing our mothers' authority will restore our humanity. From there, we will regain our identities by recognizing each other's identities. This shall be done through the Two Row Wampum process in which the identity of the original peoples of Turtle Island will be respected and officially recognized, since the original peoples' role is to protect and defend the Earth. Moreover, by removing male dominance and re-establishing the balance of matrilineal authority, our humanity could then activate itself to repair the harm we have caused to our Mother Earth.

The destruction of our environment is a result of a dysfunctional thought process. Nevertheless, if we base our decision process on the Great Law of Peace, all of our decisions will be proper for the environment. By engaging in the Two Row Wampum, we can then share the knowledge of the Great Law of Peace with the rest of the world.

We are presently at the end of a process that our Chiefs and Clan Mothers envisioned 150 years ago. They had seen that, because of the genocide inflicted upon the original peoples of Turtle Island, our knowledge of the Great Law of Peace was being destroyed, which is equivalent to what the Spanish did to Mayan knowledge. Subsequently, our elders began a written version of the Great Law. However, since at that time none of our people knew how to write in any language, the Law was written and translated by a non-Native, influenced by religious male dominance.

Today, we have just completed revising the Law in its entirety and we are translating it into English, French, Spanish and other languages. This process will culminate in a Law Recital in the Longhouse, where this written version of the Great Law of Peace will be offered as solution to the chaos that man has caused in this world.

To conclude, the Great Law of Peace is the medicine that the people need in order to heal themselves and to nurse our Mother

Earth back to health. Because destructive forces are currently waging war against our Mother Earth, driving her to the brink of death, and because all the peoples of the world are also consumed by such destructive forces, we have concluded that our only option is to fulfill our responsibility as True Beings in actively defending the Great Law of Peace against these acts of aggression. We must remind humanity of the knowledge on how to once again live in balance with our Mother Earth through the natural Laws of Creation: *Kaianerahsere`ko:wa ne skennen*. We extend this invitation to all peoples of the world to enter into this commitment and to stand with us in defence of our Mother.

Katsitenserio

Stuart Myiow Junior

Tekenitehio Hate
The Two Row Wampum

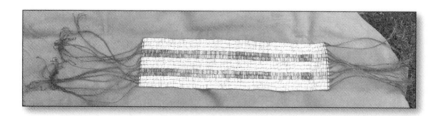

When the corrupt man from across the great waters came to Turtle Island with his ways of hatred and war, he found himself in a war different from any that he had ever known. Though he still battled his old adversaries from his homeland, as he had always done, he was now in a battle with the True Beings of Turtle Island. The white man found that these people fought for reasons different from his. He found that they had a strong social and governmental structure that made them virtually unbeatable.

Consequently, each different type of white man that came here found himself in a situation in which the victory would be impossible, given that he had old adversaries on one side and new ones on the other. The white men eventually came to realize that they would all be vulnerable to the Native Peoples if they did not make peace with us. Being that our people had offered peace to them right from the moment they set foot on Turtle Island, they were finally compelled to accept the Great Peace of the Two Row Wampum from the Chiefs of the Five Nations Confederacy.

Unfortunately, all throughout European history, the white man has never had the ways of peace inside him. Therefore he was unable then, as he is now, to understand us and the meaning of this peace treaty, just as our people could not understand his ways of hatred and war.

The beauty of the Two Row Wampum is that it contains the power to reconcile the two different ways of life and bind them together in peace. Otherwise, the two adversaries would have been locked in battle until they destroyed each other. This is the magic of the Two Row Wampum.

Some say that treaties are just contracts, and that contracts are made to be broken. This is a good analogy of a contract that is made between individuals for their own personal interests. However, what the white man has never understood (and which is leading to his downfall) is that the Two Row Wampum was not made with the personal interests of individuals or of any society, but rather for the benefit of the future generations of all races, on behalf of all Creation.

On our side, the Two Row Wampum was not conceived as a physical, tangible thing, but rather as an ideal that our people have always held: to live as a part of Creation within its laws to protect her. This has always been the belief of our people, and therefore our spirit conducts itself in this manner.

The other side of this treaty is rooted in the beliefs of the white man, which come from his government and that promote personal wealth at the expense of Creation. The treaty is also rooted in his religion that states in the book of Genesis that: "Man has dominion over Creation." These two elements lead him to believe that he has "the god-given right" to do whatever he wants to with Creation. This is further reinforced and justified through his government, which permits such conduct. The spirit of the white man uses and destroys.

Therefore, the Two Row Wampum was made between two different spirits. One has the spiritual beliefs of living within and respecting the Laws of Creation, while the other believes that it is above Creation and that it has the right to use and do whatever it wants to everything within Creation, which includes other people who do not accept its ways and beliefs. Therefore, the Two Row Wampum was an agreement between two opposing spirits for the purpose of creating a balance between human representatives.

Naturally, everyone will automatically say this sounds like a fairytale but life itself is not a fairytale. However, even modern science will substantiate that all life was created by an eternal struggle between two powers: strong and weak, hot and cold, life and death, good and evil.

Non-Natives probably won't be happy representing the evil side, but as long as the two sides keep the balance in order, neither is truly evil. Only if one deliberately, renounces its place in the balance, does it become truly evil. Even just "good" on its own is evil, for it creates an imbalance. It is important for both sides to remain true to the balance. This way, no one side can be called evil.

However, early Jesuits wrote of our people that we were the closest thing to godliness they'd ever seen. This simply meant that we lived as they thought their god would live if their god took on human form. This says a lot. Their own history clearly demonstrates that non-Natives live exactly opposite to the way their god would live if their god took on human form. Even their religion states that man was created in the image of god. Then, what are they if they live opposite to the god in whose image they were created? History speaks for itself about who is who.

Since the Two Row Wampum Treaty was made between two specific powers, looking at the history of man right up until today clearly defines the purpose of this treaty that binds these two powers as one, in balance with each other. The roles are clear; one destroys while the other defends; one offers war, the other offers peace. The Two Row Wampum represents a common ground. It states that "we will share the land equally and none will take more than they need. Also neither shall interfere with the other's government (role in life), for this will disrupt the balance."

Nevertheless, the Earth is exploited in a process that destroys her. According to the treaty, those who exploit must give an equal share to the other party. This is not so the other party can misuse it, but so they can replenish it and put it back into our Mother Earth, repairing the initial act of destruction. In this way, the balance is preserved. Here's an example: Industry digs minerals out of our Mother Earth in a destructive way to build gasoline engines that further pollute and destroy. According to the treaty, the leaders of this industry must give a percentage to our leaders because they exploit minerals on our land. In turn, we invest the capitol in a technology that would create an engine that would run on something as simple as water (such technology already exists), thereby eliminating further pollution. Science would correct destructive acts and keep things in balance instead of developing today's nano-technologies that destroy everything.

Thus, by working as equal partners, everything can evolve together safely, rallying technology and conscience. However, this kind of protective approach only takes place within the parameters of the Two Row Wampum, for in non-Native society big business has created patent laws that give them the right to "own" ideas such as the idea of a water-powered engine. Even though such technology exists, it will never be utilized, because big business would lose millions of dollars on oil-based products, millions of dollars on pollution control devices that they build themselves and sell in the gas engine market, millions of dollars in the service of the industry, not to mention the millions of dollars big business (including the government) would have to spend to re-educate millions of people, as the workforce would shift into environmentally conscious business within a new cleaner, safer industry. Consequently, humanity will never be able to save itself.

However, within the Two Row Wampum, our people are not subject to the non-Native laws of patents and red tape that big business uses to prevent such technology from being developed.

Thanks to our immunity to their system, we could easily entice the world's top scientists with the lure of not only the privilege of being part of such a revolution, but also with the lure of being tax-exempt on the earnings they would make while in our employ—something everyone could agree on.

Naturally, people might think this a grandiose vision, an unattainable fairytale, but then, what other viable option is there? When we consider where the present technology is taking us and how it makes us all live in anxiety, either we, as humans, are going to blow a fuse, or the engine room of nanotechnologies is going to blow up in our faces. If we do not make the dire changes needed, our people and the other humans on this planet are headed for a breakdown.

Nobody would ever believe—except for environmentalists, governments, and modern science—that we could predict the future this easily. However, most people (Natives and non-Natives) can feel an uneasiness, like when a little kid does something wrong and tries to hide while watching over his shoulder, knowing he will be punished.

One time, in a public meeting here in Kahnawake when I spoke about the Longhouse and the Two Row Wampum, the mayor told me: "That sounds good, but it's all in your head. I wish I could get in there but I have to live in the real world." This was evident enough that it is not only the white man who is breaking the Two Row Wampum, but so are those who we call "our own people." To switch sides goes against the agreement. It is illegal to leave one's post, and the one who does becomes truly evil. Moreover, we would have to be complete idiots to accept that putting guns to our head and pulling the trigger (as the white man does) is the only one true reality. There is always an alternative. The Two Row Wampum just happens to be the only alternative. It would solve all our political and social problems (for Natives and non-Natives) just as it once did for our ancestors. It would put everything in its place and bring order back to Creation.

Nevertheless, there is a problem of imposter Natives who misrepresent reality. The elected band councils try but will never be able to access or negotiate the Two Row Wampum like they pretend, for they've already joined the other side. This makes them a danger to our people and all Creation as well. Their charade misrepresents the Two Row Wampum and hinders its true purpose from taking place.

In January 1994, the Minister of Indian Affairs said during a parliamentary debate that Aboriginal Self-Government[14] was based on the Two Row Wampum Treaty. However, what needs to be understood is that this Wampum was established according to the Great Law of Peace of the Five Nations Confederacy that decrees that *anyone who creates anything outside the Law no longer has access thereto or to its treaties.*

People involved in this supposed self-government benefit only from an imaginary power, given that they subject themselves to government authorities. Moreover, they are separated from the Great Law of Peace, which leaves them without access to the rights and obligations of the Two Row Wampum Treaty and without the right to negotiate it. So if this so-called self-government is based on the Two Row Wampum, why was it not established in negotiations with those who created this treaty: the Chiefs of the Five Nations Confederacy? Also, people outside the Confederation, although they can be under its protection, could be unfamiliar with the treaty. Finally, with the advent of Aboriginal self-government, we imperil the collective rights of our nations and we risk losing them forever.

In 1973, during the creation of the Warriors Society, we warned our people. Then, in the early 1980s, when cigarette money began to circulate, we warned them again. What did it bring us? They tried to kill us. In 1994, a law was proposed for the sale of alcohol in Kahnawake. My father, a young woman of about 20 years and I were the only ones to oppose it, arguing that by doing this we would see our community become the bar capital of all Iroquois, making

---

14. Structure under the jurisdiction of the federal government that allows Native people to supposedly control the administration of their members, their lands, resources, and related program and policies through agreements with the federal and provincial governments.

us the beginning of the cancer that would eventually destroy our people.

If we are able to identify problems in which our nation is sinking, it is not because we are smarter, it is because we stand by the Law. All the others are detached from it. When you go away from the Law, you then depend upon your own thinking, and if you are part of a group of corrupt people, your thoughts will be subject to corruption; you will not be able to discern truth from lies.

Even if we have proof of these evidences in hand, we know that it does not matter now because what is going on will happen, no matter the circumstances. The people have decided, whatever the cost, to commit suicide. My father and I are like two buffaloes forced over the buffalo jump[15] into the ravine. Though we cry out to stop, all the buffaloe behind us keep pushing ahead. We are inevitably heading for the ravine. Even if we would stop telling others that we do not intend to continue, their running would sweep us away anyway, as has happened in the past.

---

15. A buffalo jump is a place that was used by North American Indians to hunt buffalo by driving a part of a herd to jump over a cliff.

 Katsitenserio
Stuart Myiow Junior

Kastowa
The Chief Headdress

For six years, my family and I went away to Phoenix, Arizona, for there was war in Kahnawake, and the Warriors were trying to kill us. I was 15, so that was in 1978 when my family moved to save our lives. If we had stayed home, we would have been killed. They had already tried to attack my big brother and, during our absence, they attacked our Chief. When we returned from Arizona, we summoned him to a meeting. I did not appreciate what I heard. I then told my father that this man was no longer my Chief since he did not uphold the Great Law of Peace and Understanding and the Two Row Wampum.

Later, in 1985, on a Sunday evening, I was on my way to New York to go to work. I was driving alone in my car when I saw a wolf cub dead on the roadside. Then, about 500 metres away, was another cub, also dead, lying with paws in the air. Then, some 500 metres away, was the mother, dead too, paws in the air as well. I knew something was wrong. Once arrived in New York, I called my mother, who told me that the Chief—the one I said was not my Chief anymore—had died. What I had not known was that he had health problems that affected his thinking and that he was under tremendous pressure because of threats. However, when he died, I did not go to his funeral, since he was not my Chief by not having upheld the Law.

Twenty-one years later in 2006, his wife, whose health was fading, came up the hill to the Longhouse. I was working in the garden when my father called me. I had never seen her here before. We had not seen this woman since her husband had died. When I arrived, she was crying. She held a bag in her hands. I did not know what it was. Before he died, her husband, Joe, dictated what to do with the contents of this bag. He asked her to keep it until the person designated to receive it stood out from the rest of the people. This is the way she handed me the *kastowa* with a tobacco bag that belonged to her husband, saying: "This is for you." She was shaking and crying; it was an important shift for the *kastowa*.

The *kastowa* has not been passed to me according to the Law. Therefore, I do not wear it as a fully condoled[16] chief and I do not

---

16. The term "condoled" means a chief legally installed through an official ceremony.

want to make myself look like a chief, since I am not one. Anyway, anyone could find reasons why I cannot be chief. I, myself, say that I cannot be one. So, the only time I use the *kastowa* is in ceremonies, teachings and for political representations.

The *kastowa* is the Mohawk headdress bearing three upright feathers and deer antlers. It is worn by men symbolizing the chieftainship title awarded to a man by the women. However, the women have not selected me; I am not a condoled chief within the Law. Nevertheless, I'll tell you about the *kastowa* and how I legally wear it.

The *kastowa* is not the power, but it assists it. From what I have seen, I know its power is beyond an individual's capability. After the chief's headdress came here to the Longhouse, I did not start using it immediately, because I knew that I did not have the right to wear it yet. In my mind, it was given to me to hold. But as we went on applying the Law, the women were able to install the *kastowa* upon me, but it was a temporary measure.

The *kastowa* carries a symbol that identifies the family clan. On the one I wear, there is a wolf; that way, when you go into a community, you can readily identify the Chief of Clan you want to speak to.

My mother was from the same clan as our late Chief: the Wolf Clan. As someone from the Wolf Clan cannot marry a member of the same clan, when you see a woman of the Wolf Clan sitting alongside a man of the Wolf Clan, you know she is not his wife; she is as a Mother of the Clan, granting and legitimizing authority. In addition, because Clan is transmitted by the mother, I am of the Wolf Clan too.

In this world, many people might believe that a man and a woman of the same clan share the same pillow. They say "Oh! She is his wife. They sit together and they make decisions." People then think that this could influence the decisions that they are making. However, a Wolf cannot marry a Wolf. He can only marry a Bear or a Turtle, as a Bear can only marry a Wolf or a Turtle, and a Turtle, a Wolf or a Bear.

The deer, represented by the horns on the *kastowa,* is a migratory animal, like the bison or any other migratory animal. The horns of these animals act as radar that detects the magnetic field of the Earth. These are antennas. If you are a hunter, look into the eye holes in the skull of a deer. Not in his eyes but in the eye holes, in the hollows of his eyes, deep down, you'll see a tiny hole that goes straight up to the horns, small like a needle. This hole does not go all the way up to the tip of the deer antler; it goes maybe an inch (two centimetres) or something like that. These holes in the eye sockets are like a sixth sense. All horned migratory creatures are constantly receiving energy from the Earth's magnetic field, the holes act like antennae.

The Earth's magnetic field circulates through our Mother Earth's body the same way the blood does in our body. It leaves from the South Pole, reaches the North Pole and comes back to the South Pole. During its journey, it picks up what is happening on the Earth. When the magnetic field returns, it has the knowledge and the information of where and what it was previously. So the Earth's magnetic field adjusts continuously to the environment, and it is constantly giving the creatures the message of what is happening throughout Creation. That's what indicates to them where to migrate.

The monarch butterfly, which is a horned creature too, can fly from Mexico to Mohawk territory in two generations, but it flies back in only one. How does it know where to go? It receives information from the Earth's magnetic field about its journey.

When a storm is coming, the animals react beforehand, and they will know where to go. On a calm day, they could relax under an apple tree, but they could look for a better shelter if a big storm is coming. We could compare it to a plane flight where the data is recorded in the black box. All creatures have a kind of black box within the fibre of their being. The Earth's magnetic field is continuously communicating not only with horned creatures, but with us, as with every other living thing.

We have five senses, but a chief has a sixth one, thanks to the antlers on the *kastowa*. Because there is always human business that needs to have guidance or leadership, the Chief always has to be connected with what is happening within Creation. According to tradition, in everyday life, he must wear the *kastowa* during business hours (while the Sun is up). Of course, we are talking about the past; nevertheless today the Chiefs still wear the *kastowa* during ceremonies and circles.

People think that the Chief has to represent the people. They are right, but if the people are wrong, then the Chief has to represent the Law. This is the reason why he has to keep his mind in tune with his knowledge, in tune with the application of Law and up to date about everything that is happening around him and around the world, as far as possible. Today, we have the Internet, so we can gather a lot of information. In the past, communication circulated by humans; we had runners' networks that carried the news between the nations at all times.

At the Longhouse, when we started to use the *kastowa*, we almost immediately had access to information that we did not have before. There are things we know now that were almost impossible to know; knowledge that was here before 500 years ago. The *kastowa* brought us access to the Grandmother Moon teachings. This is not something that we were taught, even if they were here hundreds of years ago. None of us had ever had access to that before. This knowledge is re-emerging out of the past that is encoded in the Earth's magnetic field, and when that is combined with the *kastowa* and an individual who knows and applies the Law, these three elements together allow for the decoding and understanding of absolutely anything and everything in Creation. Anyway, when a person subjects themselves to the power within Creation, they can never make bad decisions. If you base your thinking process on the Law, anything that you will think about will never be wrong.

Even outside of the power of those mechanisms, outside of the magnetic field, of the *kastowa*, and of the individual, the chief's headdress still influences everybody who sees it. Right away, people feel and know something, and thus conduct themselves differently. They act humbly in front of it. They respect it, even if they don't know what it is. They react that way because without knowing it, they are interacting with the Earth's magnetic field, which is the spirit of our Mother Earth, constantly being renewed and kept her alive. So she has her workers who are the chieftains that hold the *kastowa*, and because of that their lives are different.

Any man who covets the chieftain title is an idiot. First thing, for a chief, the demand is so heavy, that it risks breaking anyone who tries to wear it. Moreover, if a non-eligible person grabs that title, even in just imagining it, it could kill him, because in the person's mind, it is like a fuse within an electrical circuit that blows. To carry the chieftain title, the man has to be in such balance that the women can determine that he stands out from the rest of the people. Once the man is selected, women direct him constantly to maintain the peace. So the title does not come because the man decides to be the Chief, but because the women choose him.

However, the Chief is not a person in authority. He comes from Creation in which natural selection occurs. Our Mother Earth chooses and selects the people to wear the *kastowa*; she has a pool of sons from which to select. If that pool is small, her variety of selection becomes limited and more specialized. Then she has to carefully manage her family to keep the power in balance.

Even when the Chief does not wear the *kastowa*, the horns continue to work all the time. A chief has to be in his position 24 hours a day, without any letting up. When you consider that's how it will be until his death, this represents a great burden. I have seen what happened to the man who was holding the *kastowa* before me: a lifetime of constraints. While I was seeing it, I did not know what I was looking at; I could not comprehend it. Now, looking back, I see how this man's burden consumed his strength as his people became corrupted.

Today, an ultimatum has to be directed to male dominance and the only voice available to women is through the *kastowa*. Unfortunately, we find ourselves in a crucial stage because while the *kastowa* represents one of the most ancient and important mechanisms of this world for women in terms of power and authority, it is about to disappear. No one else will be eligible to wear it throughout the Mohawk Nation. Here at our Longhouse in Kahnawake, this is the last legal *kastowa* left now.

Humanity is the star of the big show staged by our Mother Earth: the show of life. Humans are the main players in this Creation, for we can produce negative or positive changes within all Creation by our decisions. Thanks to the *kastowa*, we have access to knowledge of everything within Creation. But obviously, anybody in this world could put it on without being exposed to that power. It takes the proper combination. In fact, anybody can wear the *kastowa*, but only a person who carries the birthright (the clan) can utilize it; if not, it is like a car without the key: it will go nowhere.

The *kastowa* on its own is hanging on the wall of the Longhouse, but without the two other elements (the Earth's magnetic field and the individual that carries the birthright), it is useless. Like the Turtle, Wolf and Bear, or proton, neutron and electron, none of them exists without the other. Humans would not be the stars of the show unless they were able to fill that position: to take care of the Creation, to walk through it, not as a lord above it, but as managers and sons of our mothers.

Nowadays, given how the world works, people are forced to remain silent. There are only few people who have the right to speak. "You, are you drinking? Bah! Your words do not interest people. Ah! You! You do this or that? Nobody is interested in hearing you." I have witnessed this situation in my own people. I saw in a town meeting an elected mayor saying to a resident of Kahnawake, "Ah! Sit down and shut up! You are nothing but a drunk!" The common people have no voice as well; they are not represented. However, everyone is supposed to have a voice, but male dominance puts restrictions on that to ensure that people do not have any voice, or that their voices are filtered through a certain ideology.

We did a complete reversal in our thinking about the ones we listen to. The reality is that, among our people, most are wrong because they have adopted the ways dictated by religion, which stigmatizes us by driving us to believe that this way is the right way of thinking and anything outside of it is bad. Once someone is indoctrinated by religion, his thought is never right. Furthermore, by adopting religion as a lifestyle, the first people that we have restricted are the women.

The traumas that male dominance has caused in this world have been multiplied from each generation to the next and have never been addressed by any religion, faith, or any sitting government in the over 2,000 years of history. This situation is equivalent to breaking your leg in the morning without attending to it, and then breaking each limb as you go on throughout the day without attending to them either. How long could you go on before you have a total breakdown and are unable to function at all, or even die? If you did attend to each trauma, after a couple of days, you would have to re-break each bone in order to reset them properly.

Currently, this is the most important stage of human evolution we are at. If we are to survive, we have to re-break the bones and reset them properly. This means that all traumas inflicted on humanity and on Creation through the male dominance mentality must be acknowledged, addressed, and corrected, and our mothers must be returned to their natural seat of authority so they can return identity to the people and manage our nations with love once again.

Everyone might automatically think that this is a utopian pipedream. Well, if peace is a dream, look at your reality of war and what it is doing to our Mother Earth: The beauty of Creation is being destroyed. We cannot allow this to happen. We must reach back into our true identities and take back control of the legacy we are leaving to our children. Presently, we are cocking the gun, putting it into our children's hands, aiming it at their heads, and teasing the trigger. We have sealed the fate of our children, all the faces yet beneath the Earth (future generations) are doomed to destruction. We all know this is the truth of what is happening, and if we do nothing to change the situation, we are killing our own children.

The women must take back their power and start to do the very thing they were once killed for in the first place[17]: their Moon

---

17. This refers to witch hunts.

Ceremonies. They have to return to their Women's Council Fire[18] from where they can have control of and manage their families once again. They have to return identity and respect back to the people; remove war and corruption and replace it with the love that a mother has for her children. Our mothers must be returned back to power as the authority of our nations.

It is for this reason that I wear the *kastowa*: to convey this message to all.

---

18. This refers to the fact that the Councils often took place around the fire, where people gathered.

Katsitenserio

Stuart Myiow Junior

Noh'naken:kha Kowanen Katsenhaien
After the Last Great Council

When we work in council, we put our knowledge together with the rest of the people's minds to make one collective. So, we can determine in advance between us what is the truth, what is wrong, what we are going to do, what is our policy on this or that. We have policies on absolutely everything. When the people know the *Kaianerahsere'kó:wa ne skennen* (the Great Law of Peace and Understanding) and know their responsibilities to the Council, then you have a predetermined position, but it is not *your* position. And if you base your decisions on the Law, then you can never go wrong, and you become an enemy to the enemies of the Earth.

In ceremonies, we speak to give thanks, but in council, we speak to make decisions. There, our words are part of policies that are put into action for the people and for the environment in which we live; they are less personal, making the Council the important event of Creation.

Within the Five Nations Confederacy, for over 2000 years, every decision was made through the Council. First, we have the

Women's Council Fire[19] which is the primary Council Fire; then, we have the Male Council Fire; then, we have the Council Fires of the Turtle, Wolf, and Bear for the women and for the men too (each on their own), followed by the Turtle, Wolf and Bear for the women and the men grouped together. After that, we have the General People's Council, then the Nation Council and from there, we go to the biggest Council: the Grand Council of the Five Nations, where the nations sit together representing all the clans, all the people, and the unbroken lineage of Sky Woman, Grandmother Moon, our Mother Earth, and on to all the women.

I consider myself to be extremely fortunate, because I have seen the last Council Fire, and I spoke within the last legal Grand Council at Onentake after my mother, who was on her deathbed, told us to go there. For me, it was something that was very important; at 27 years old, to speak on the floor of the Grand Council. This means I have talked to Elders, to Chiefs and to Clan Mothers, many of whom have been in their position for decades. In council, you are in the center of consciousness and righteousness where only what is right, true, good, and proper is spoken. However, at this council, *kanikonraksa* ("the Bad Mind") was introduced, which led the Nation Council on the wrong path. Therefore, it was the last Grand Council.

Imagine what our nations are missing! Imagine what human beings no longer have access to! It is like saying that you are a carpenter, but you don't have any hammer and nails anymore. Here, we can see the necessity for something from the past to come back to us. And this is where you get the male dominant idiots who say: "Ah! You live in the past! We cannot live in the past. Do you want us to go back to live in tepees?" For me, these words are like if we are in a life or death situation, and we have to accept death. If the only solution is in the past, well, we should apply that. These people say that we live in modern days, and that we cannot use something that is old like the council process in this present time. But that is not the past. The negative is the past; the positive is the

19. See note 18, page 81.

future, and the answers to what is happening to us may look like they are in the past, but they are in the future.

There is only one thing that is going to keep us alive, and we know what it is, and we have to make it happen. If only a couple of people sit together and talk, they will never make it happen by themselves. Anybody can find excuses: "Oh! I am too small, the job is too big, I am only one person, what could I do?" We defeat ourselves before we even start to take action. This is why Mohawks do not look at what we cannot do: We look at what must be done, and then we do it. And if it is not yet done in our lifetime, then our children will do it. And if it is not in their time, then their children will do it. But if I do not start now, then my children will never fulfill it, and my grandchildren will never do it either, and that would make me corrupt in addition to being useless to our Mother Earth in the present threatening situation.

The inaction in front of what everybody is doing right now drives everyone, by definition, to be corrupt. Everybody is actually the enemy of our Mother Earth until we get on the right side of the line. This is where real women and real men exist and take real actions. And real women will take real actions and they will not allow poor excuses for men to continue to conduct themselves in the way that they are doing it in this world. Something has been lost, but we are going to get it back, no matter how long it takes or what has to be done to get it back.

I know that my mother did not bring me into this world for nothing; she brought me in for a purpose, and I know what role she played in this world: She was the last legal Clan Mother of the Mohawk Nation. I know what she was representing, and there is no way that I am going to let that down. The job that she put us here for will be done. Male dominance, destruction and trauma are going to be ripped from this world, but you must help us; you have to hold up your end of the bargain here. This bargain was made within your own mind. Either we remain human, or we are not going to be human anymore.

If you are fortunate enough to still have your mother, tell her how much you love her. Touch her face; touch her hair. Tell her how beautiful she is. Get to know her in the same way that you are supposed to know and take care of Mother Earth. Tell your mother how important she is to you. The life that you have, everything that you have, is thanks to her. Tell her how much you appreciate it. Honour her in the same way she has honoured you, by giving you life, and bring peace to her heart. The mother is the primary thing in this world. By doing this, you show that example to your kids and to your friends. Do it openly and do not be afraid, do not be shy, and when there are many people around, that is the time to do it more. In many ways, all people are medicines. Sometimes, people say that we are helping them, but they are helping us too. We are all medicines to each other.

Since my sons came into this world, I have been kissing them, right up until now. Every time I see them, I kiss them. They are at that stage now where they are ashamed, where they don't want people to see that. Well, we are guys. Sometimes, when we are in front of people and I kiss my boys who are taller than I am on the lips, people might wonder: "Hey, what is going on there?" Don't be afraid of that. Don't shy away and show the example by making those things happen. I did not get that from my father, because we are from that generation where a break was inflicted on people through the residential schools[20] and all of those things. This is why I did not get to know my father the same way that my boys know me. It is something that I had to make happen.

When the fetus is growing, the first thing that is created is the spirit which is given through the act of love that comes from the mother, and the first part of the body that starts to grow is the heart. Legs are going to grow too, but in order for them to grow, they need blood. This is why the first thing that grows is the heart,

---

20. Residential schools were public boarding schools intended for Native Americans in Canada. Endorsed by the Department of Indian Affairs, they spearheaded the schooling, evangelism and assimilation of Aboriginal children. This practice, which separated children from their families, has been described by some as a cultural genocide resulting in the expression "kill the Indian in the heart of the child." These schools existed from the 1820s to the 1990s. The last one closed in 1996.

so the blood starts circulating. The spirit comes from Sky Woman, the blood comes from our Grandmother Moon, and the body comes from our Mother Earth. These things have to be remembered by everybody; we have to tell the people about that reality of Creation. Moreover, we won't be able to continue to talk the way we do if you don't do it with us. If we want to move, we need to walk with our two legs, if not, we are not going to go anywhere. The message we carry must be said everyday to everybody.

Rorahkwaieshon

Rorahkwaieshon Myiow

As'kànik'tshera
Hope

My name is Rorahkwaieshon, which means "Our Grand-mother Moon smiles upon him." I am the second and youngest son of Stuart Junior. I am from the Bear Clan "hung about the neck." This means that I have been adopted by the Bear Clan, because my mother has no clan that she could transmit to me. In this circumstance, I cannot become a chief of my clan, but if I have children with a woman who transmits a clan to them, they, in turn, will have the possibility to become chief of their clan. As a 16-year-old Mohawk boy, I go to school with non-Native people and I don't really feel any difference between us. Of course, there is my name. When the teachers check attendance in the classroom for the first time, I feel that I am a little different, but that is okay. I usually help the people by telling them my nickname, Eshon, so it is easier for everyone.

At school, I study French, so I can understand it a little. I am now at Secondary V level of schooling. Later, I plan to go to college to study dentistry. This field of study sounds interesting to me and I know that it could lead me to obtain a good job. Because I made that career choice, I am studying science. And obviously after college, I will have to go to university too, but I feel very fine with that.

Actually in my teenage life, when I imagine the future, I don't think I will have children. Maybe I will change my mind later, but this is the way I see things for the moment. I will perhaps still get married, and it does not really matter if my wife is a Native or not. For me, when I have a love relationship, it is not a priority to be with a Native girl; my priority is to be with a girl whom I love. For the moment, I am not looking for a girlfriend. I enjoy life while playing video games, and I am satisfied with that.

When I think about the things that are destroying our Mother Earth, I am concerned. As everybody does, I don't know exactly what is going to happen in the future, but I feel that things have to change if we want to have a good life, for us, and for the next generations. If I had the power to change something wrong right away, my priority would be the water pollution because it is very important. If we had no more water, life would be impossible . . .

At the Longhouse, my home, when we have ceremonies and I sing our traditional songs—keeping the beat with the turtle shells on our old bench with my dad—I feel good. I like that, because I feel connected with my family: my father, my grandfather and my brother. I cherish these moments. Even if my adult life leads me to leave the Longhouse one day or another, I will always come back and I know my heart will be there forever, because this is where our tradition is transmitted to me. These are my roots, and this is the most important thing to keep in mind as a young Mohawk man.

Their mother sings about everything in Creation.

Taionterah'kwatahsawen
First Quarter

Women Words

From five different origins, these Native women
are the mothers of our nations. Their voices unite to carry
a message of hope and life.

Kaneratentha

Kaneratentha Cross

Taieh'wisats'teke Tsinine Ia'kon'kwe Kanienke'ha'ka
Resilience of a Kanienke'ha'ka Woman

My family calls me Tentha. I am Mohawk and I live in Kahnawake. I was born on my cousin's wedding day. Three months later, I received my name, Kaneratentha, at the Longhouse. It means: "She drops the leaves." I grew up from a very young age according to the teachings of the Longhouse. With the Mohawks, women transmit the clans. Since my great-great-grandmother was French, the line was interrupted, and women who followed did not receive and cannot transmit any clan. My daughter and I therefore find ourselves under the protection of the Bear Clan. Not that it is bad, but this affects me, because in the *Kanienke'ha'ka* Nation, the clans are strong families and I am only under the protection of a clan without being a part of it officially.

Being a woman without a *Kanienke'ha'ka* clan represents a major difficulty for me. Other women in the nation who have a clan perceive things differently, which regularly generates conflicts. All this hurts me because I feel separated, even if I know that I am not apart. I feel that I have to constantly overcome my feelings, my perceptions, in order to stand up, to ground myself, to be strong and to find peace.

Shortly after my birth, because of the economic situation of the time, men had to go away to work in order to provide for their families. My grandfather on my father's side was already an iron worker in Brooklyn. My father followed him there to work, and we all went to live there as well.

After having gone to Brooklyn, my father and my mother divorced when I was only two or three years old. I do not know exactly what happened, but my mother returned to Kahnawake. My brother and I had not seen her for years. Because my father worked all the time, my grandmother, who was also in Brooklyn, took care of us. My brother was just a baby at that time. When you're a child, you are not aware of the situation, but you feel abandoned. We cried all the time to see our mother.

When my father died at the age of 27, I was 5 years old. With my grandmother, we came back to live in Kahnawake. She went through this with difficulty and she told us that we had to return to live with our mother. So one day in May, my mother took us with her. We did not want to because we felt that we did not know her.

I then spent a lot of time with my aunt Marilyn, my paternal grandmother's sister, although I did not want to abandon my mother. It was a strange feeling. I felt disloyal to my mother, but I stayed with my aunt. I was sleeping and eating with her; I went to school in the morning from her home. Aunt Marilyn was like a mother to me. Besides, I had several women who were mothers to me. I consider myself lucky to have had all this love.

Because my aunt was a woman of the Longhouse, she spent a lot of time there. I followed her in ceremonies or in all that was happening there. This is one of the most beautiful moments of my childhood, a memory I cherish. Without it, I think I would not have had the opportunity to live by the Great Law of Peace, because neither my grandmother nor my mother took part in the Longhouse as much as my aunt did.

When I was nine, Marilyn suffered from a stroke that left her with many impairments. She was paralyzed and had to relearn everything: scratching, talking, eating, moving and walking—everything. I remember visiting and feeding her in the hospital. It was unbearable for me. It was another event that broke my heart. I was so young and I had had my heart broken so many times.

During my teenage time, I went to high school in Kahnawake and it was very hard. Everyone here is strong and hardened, even the girls from an early age. You have to stand up for yourself here. Then one day, when I was 15, my mother was ousted by the Kahnawake Band Council after she and her partner had had a baby. Her partner is not Mohawk. He grew up here; his father is Mohawk, but his mother is white. So we had to move to the city.

I suffered a great cultural shock from being torn from my roots to live and attend school in Côte-des-Neiges.[21] I held out for a month, but I ended up rebelling. I then told my mother that I was coming back to live in Kahnawake. I was determined to find a way to survive, so at 15, I rented a house with my brother who is a year my junior, and who felt like me and also wanted to return to Kahnawake. I went back to school with a scholarship of $700 per month; which allowed me to pay the rent that was not too expensive and to take care of my brother and myself.

Later, I met the soon-to-be father of my child. I was 17 and he was 20. I quickly became pregnant and gave birth to my daughter at 18 years old. I remember the day she was born, I held her in my arms looking through the window on this beautiful autumn morning. Then I chose her name: Autumn. I also promised her with all my heart that I would be there for her, no matter what the circumstances were.

Her father and I were still young, and he had not changed anything in his life, despite becoming a father. I needed his help, but I think it was too much pressure for him. So I told him if he could not be a father, he could not stay with us. From that moment, I was determined to be a good mother, even if I was alone to take

21. Multi-ethnic neighbourhood of Montréal.

care of my child, and I assumed my responsibilities. Although there have been people to teach me things, I learned my mother role by myself largely because I was firmly connected to my daughter. At that time, I left school and I lived on social assistance for a while. My brother was still with us and his passion for music saved him. He found the meaning of his life by creating music. It's amazing to see where he is and how he lives today. It makes me happy.

Four years after the birth of my daughter, I moved to Lachine[22], because a woman offered me a job in an international video conference company, even though I had absolutely no experience, and I did not speak French. This woman offered me the job simply because she liked me. I worked full-time for this company for 12 years.

I learned a lot in this job. They even invited me to be part of the management team. However, I was constantly torn between work and home, because all this time I was at work, so I did not take care of my child. Unless you have relatives who tell you "Okay, you can live with us and you have nothing to pay," you do not have the choice to meet your needs and those of your child, and anyway, there is always a price to pay even when they tell you that you have nothing to pay. I had too much pride to count on anyone else to take care of my daughter and myself. Nevertheless, with this work, I was running around all of the time. In the evening, I was preparing for the next day, and on weekends, I was preparing for the next week.

Obviously, Autumn went to school outside of Kahnawake. She met lots of kids, which I find fantastic, and she learned both languages: English and French. However, at one point, she no longer felt happy in school. She couldn't find her place there. We had a great discussion, she and I, and I took her out from the school system to have her home-schooled from the age of 13. Since that day, she thanks me because I let her choose her own path. She is beautiful and well-rooted in her life.

---

22. City in suburban Montréal.

A time came when I wanted to build a house, *my* house. Normally, what people do is that they hire a contractor. For my part, I chose to go and live with my mother for a moment, then with my grandmother, and during that time I saved enough money to start the project. I did my research without referring to a contractor. I thought that I could do it by myself. Not that I took a hammer to build my house alone, but I managed the entire project. It was a big challenge. I hired workers who did the work. I knew what I wanted and I got it. I wanted to make my own decisions without someone trying to influence me. Today I have my own house in a quiet place in the forest. I chose a place I could live in balance with nature. My water comes from a well; I am not connected to any other water system. I also managed to preserve some trees around my house, which is important to me.

For the last five years I have had a boyfriend, but we recently separated. It was my choice because I felt I was losing my balance through that relationship. This is my quest right now: Find and preserve the balance through a relationship with a man, even when one of us is out of balance.

The relationship we had made me feel very negative, which is something I do not want to experience. So I told my companion that I needed my space back, and then he moved out. Since he left, I have the incredible sense of having found my feminine power. I feel in full possession of my faculties, as if I am able to discern better what I need as a woman, and my needs are now a priority. It took me five years, but finally I understood. I do not want to be alone for the rest of my life; I just want to live with someone who can live in balance with me.

Being a woman is hard. Being Mohawk is hard. Being a single mother is hard. Providing for family and cultivating happiness at the same time is hard. Just being in this world at this time is hard. Like a tree which faces the storms, we must keep our roots deeply planted in the Earth to avoid falling. We have to stay strong. I see myself as a tree shaken by the wind. Often I have wanted to give up, but instead of turning my attention to the negative side, I am grateful and see the beautiful things. But, also, I continue pressing forward in my beliefs and learnings that strengthen me, my daughter, the women and men, our Mother Earth, Grandmother Moon, and all things living and breathing life, so we can live peacefully and in balance with one another.

Today, I work at the Mohawk Bingo. That's enough. I do not need to accumulate tons of money. I just need to take part in the Longhouse and to live in freedom, happiness and serenity. Finally, I have come to this point where I have gone through many difficulties and I am now exactly where I want to be.

Messinak Kassutasset
Marie-Émilie Lacroix

Takunishishkueu
Medicine Woman

Messinak Kassutasset, meaning "Persevering Turtle" is my name in the language of my people. Marie-Émilie Lacroix is the one assigned to me by whites with whom I grew up. I was born in Uepishtikueiau, in an orphanage, and was adopted a few months later. I have the happiness of being a teacher in a secondary school, a medicine woman, the mother of five children and the grandmother of seven grandchildren.

I am an Innu woman (Montagnais) who comes from a childhood of abuse, violence and suffering. I am a fatherless child with no land. My roots are deeply Native even without papers. I am a *deculturized* human among others. I consider myself to be "Indian"[23], without being able to prove it. I found my origins in my thirties by looking for traces of my family here and there.

Prior to 1985, an Indian woman who married a man from another culture lost her Indian status. On the other hand, a Native *man* who married a *woman* from another community did not lose anything and this woman received the indigenous status of her husband. However, at the adoption of Bill C-31, this discrimination was abolished, or rather transferred to the second generation. Indeed, a child born from an Aboriginal mother will

---

23. Word used formerly to describe Amerindians.

be the last Indian of the line if the father is not Native. The next generations will not be recognized as indigenous. However, a child born from a non-Indian mother may transmit his or her Aboriginal status for at least a generation if the father is Aboriginal.

As for me, I simply have no identity. Neither white nor Indian, who am I? Born of a single mother, people told me they did not know any details about my background and about my adoption. Lies! They know the truth but refuse to speak. Anyway, a child born from an unknown father is automatically considered to be a non-Native.

Nevertheless, according to the Great Law of Peace, among the Mohawks, the lineage is transmitted by the mother. So when the mother is Mohawk, no matter who the father is, the child is Mohawk. If I refer to this law, knowing that my mother is Innu, I could say that I am not a crossbreed, but purely Innu.

When I was a child, people insulted me and I didn't understand what my attackers meant until, at 10 years, I looked up the word "bastard" in the dictionary. Within the ranks of my adoptive family, no one knew that at the age of three or four I spent long days locked in the cellar, where I was assailed by fear.

A young uncle, in my adoptive family, was the first man to abuse me. When I wanted to get help, they reprimanded me: "You have to say nothing; otherwise you'll break the family! It is you who tempted him, you're so needy! You cannot stop men; a man is a man! Shut up with your nonsense!" And the worst lie of all: "When you get married, you will have forgotten."

This uncle, who remained free and without remorse, was the first of a too-long-line of people who were close to me and, with their hands, created a rift in the current of my life. Despite the fact that I have been abused many times, with courage, one step at a time, I have resurfaced and avoided sinking.

Resilient after these difficulties, I still undertook major projects. I had the determination to get a Bachelor of Education in 1975, a second one in social work in 1982, and an ESL teaching certificate in 2008. Moreover, with the help of a young mother, I set up, in Québec City, La Leche League, whose mission is to promote breastfeeding and help mothers to breastfeed their babies. I was also a caterer of vegetarian cooking, and started (with two other teachers) a small private school in a large country house. The children rode in carts, worked in the garden and had access to a forest for science work. Finally, for 25 years, I had the privilege to be a midwife accompanying women who chose to give birth at home. While home-schooling, I drove long distances regularly around the province along with my children, who tagged along with their schoolwork.

I was a midwife for many years when I decided I would give birth to my third child at home by myself. A few months before her birth, I had assisted a mother whose baby was born in his amniotic sac, which is very rare. It was beautiful. Two months later, in May, my baby arrived. I gave birth alone in my room. Everything was fine, I was squatting and I pushed, and then my daughter was born in her amniotic sac too. I punctured the membrane and she came out as if she slipped on a river. That child is so quiet and peaceful. Nothing bothers her in life.

Some months later, I helped a friend to give birth, but the day after, the placenta had not come out. So I drove her to the hospital to undergo curettage. The mother was quickly supported by the medical team, while I stayed with her newborn baby and my own baby. Indeed, when I was helping women to give birth, I took my children with me, because I sometimes left home for a long time and was breastfeeding. At one point, my friend's newborn started to cry. I did not know what to do. I did not want to breastfeed the child without the consent of her mother, but she was screaming so hungrily. Finally, I fed the baby and, at the same time, my own daughter, refusing to share her mother, also began to cry. I then found myself breastfeeding two babies simultaneously. Today, our two girls are best friends.

I was always told that a midwife never delivers her own daughter's baby because too many emotions are at play between a mother and her daughter. Yet, my pregnant daughter did not go to the hospital, and she needed someone to help her give birth. I was at her home waiting for the baby when one night I heard her shout "Mummy!" It was time. My daughter spent the night giving birth and in the early morning, the child was born. As the Sun rose and a fire burned in the fireplace, a great blue heron took flight. What a nice welcome omen for Maya! I have developed a wonderful relationship with my granddaughter.

As a social worker, I do not denigrate the work these people are doing in Native communities. However, they have to implement laws that do not correspond to our values and our traditions. According to the white culture, the therapist guides the client towards solutions. With Native people, this caregiver should keep in mind that he doesn't have before him a customer or a patient but an equal human. No one between these two is an expert. We are all on a path of healing; we learn from each other.

The return to tradition, staying in the woods, the sweat lodge, and any kind of circles are our methods. These are different but effective. Moreover, spirituality and ceremonies occupy a large place in the healing process. They can be considered as equivalent to psychiatry, psychology and even to medication in some cases. We have tales, legends, teachings of the elders, oral traditions, rituals, dances, circles, wheels. We are not lacking. One must not believe that the methods of the great schools are the only effective ones.

Despite my professional achievements, I had death in my heart for a long time, because from my birth I was diverted from my culture, my people. After being at a Native meeting, I come back home sad. In 2005, I attended a gathering of elders on the banks of the Moisie river. When I left the camp, I cried all the way from Sept-Iles through to Québec[24]. I felt like a child torn from her mother, even if I have never known mine.

---

24. More than 700 kilometers separate Sept-Iles and Québec, about eight hours by car.

Although I have often wanted to die, my attempts have failed[25]. I'm glad not to be dead. I would have missed all these pleasures that have been sprinkled on my path for several years.

A few weeks later, I discovered that I was not the only one to experience this shock. I went to Wendake, the Wendat community closer to me, and I met people who were weeping the same pain as mine, that pain, among others, of not being able to speak and understand the language.

Too many Native children have lived in residential schools[26] where they were mistreated, abused mentally and often sexually. They were brought as far as possible from their village to prevent them from walking back home. Their families were left to themselves, deprived of their children, for 10 years or more. Parents sometimes sank into depression. The stated purpose of these schools was to kill the Indian in the native child. There would be more than 4,000 Native children who died in these schools, and the bodies have not all been handed over to their families. Snatching children from their parents, their culture, and their traditions, forcing them to live like whites has weakened the generations: present and future. Residential schools were closed in 1996 because they were becoming a stain upon the government image.

I am very involved in the Native community, especially since I lived for three years in Chisasibi, at the James Bay. I have mainly worked to stop violence against women in addition to my teaching job. Before going to the interview for this job, I breastfed my baby to prevent him from being hungry during the interview and I brought him with me, not knowing how long it would last. In the room, I found myself in front of the director and the parents'

---

25. Suicide and self-inflicted injuries are the leading causes of death for First Nations youth and adults up to 44 years of age. First Nations youth commit suicide about five to six times more often than non-Aboriginal youth. The suicide rate for First Nations males is 126 per 100,000 compared to 24 per 100,000 for non-Aboriginal males. For First Nations females, the suicide rate is 35 per 100,000 compared to only 5 per 100,000 for non-Aboriginal females. Suicide rates for Inuit youth are among the highest in the world, at 11 times the national average (http://www.hc-sc.gc.ca/fniah-spnia/promotion/mental/index-fra.php). Statistics Canada.
26. See note 20, page 86.

committee: about 15 Cree[27]. As the interview was long, my baby started to look for my breast. Understanding the situation, the director ended the interview. I told myself that if I had this job, it would be a miracle. A few days later, I was informed that I had the job. So I moved to James Bay with my kids. Once there, I met the director who said, laughing: "You did not have to say a word to be hired. When they saw you with the baby, they knew you were one of them."

I taught in Chisasibi for three years. During this time I began to do social work as a private practice. I was also a midwife, which greatly annoyed the woman doctor there. She never asked her patients' opinion. She treated them as if they were bodies that had nothing to say and nothing to do. I tried to make her understand that patients are women with their own bodies and their own children, we need to give explanations and ask their permission before administering treatment. I intervened between the doctor and the mothers, which the medical community there had not been used to.

In the same period, another woman and I got a grant and we founded a newspaper. We also started to make circles of women and demonstrations against drug abuse and to stop violence against women.

During the last year there, a colleague sexually abused two of my students. I had always educated my students about these types of abuses. I met the parents of the girls and we agreed that legal action would be taken. I did my investigation in the village. Toward the end of the year, I filled a bus with 32 women who had been abused by him and we went to the inquiry of the teachers union in Radisson. He obviously lost the right to teach. Once returned to the village, I wanted to leave my evidence with the police. They refused and warned me to keep quiet at the risk of no longer having my protection guaranteed.

Meanwhile, villagers turned to me to denounce other abuses.

---

27. Aboriginal people of the North.

I could not do anything, especially because some cases were Inuit[28], and Cree police officers didn't care about the Inuit. I had no cooperation from the authorities. I came to fear for the safety of my children and I left the village, abandoning the legal proceedings.

In 2014, a study of the last 30 years revealed that around 1,200 Canadian Aboriginal women are missing and probably murdered. Proportionally, if we applied this ratio to the white population, this would amount to 35,000 Canadians or to 8,250 Quebecers.

The government doesn't intervene. The inquiry commission, which would reveal what the authorities would like to remain unknown, has been refused. It's a big injustice that strengthens prejudices, including the one that we are not as important as the rest of Canadian women. Indigenous women undoubtedly have the same human rights as other Canadians. We all know that when a white woman disappears, a search is promptly initiated.

Anyone's life has value regardless of where it is on Earth. Is not Canada a land of freedom and equality? Moreover, its government has been denounced in Geneva for negligence towards our people. Some reservations are even being compared to the Third World. I do not like this expression, but when I see what is happening in Kitcisakik[29] I am obliged to accept it, since it is not rare that a residence has no running water or electricity, is poorly insulated or that food is unavailable.

Lured by the South and to escape the difficult conditions in their communities, women, including teenagers, hitchhike out of the isolated northern communities and become easy prey. However I note, with a mixture of joy and caution, that more and more media are informing the public about the subject. Also, with a project such as the Plan Nord, we fear an increase in the rate of prostitution, as has happened in the past. Many juicy stories have circulated, told by men bragging of their sexual exploits, hinting that the girls were not necessarily consenting.

28. Aboriginal people of the Far North.
29. Native reserve in northern Québec.

Nevertheless, more and more whites are interested in our culture and do not hesitate to come and experience our ceremonies. For many, their ignorance about our history hurts them. Some excuse themselves and feel a deep unease at the suffering inflicted upon us. This solidarity comforts. Will the time of colonization finally end? We have a prayer that expresses great wisdom: "O Great Spirit give me the wisdom not to judge my neighbor without having spent 10 days in his moccasins."

Last year, I traveled to Haiti to perform humanitarian work. I lived with the natives there. We connected right away. We recognize each other because we have lived through common struggles. I also felt that we have developed the same forces through these events that our people have faced.

For several years, I have delighted in sharing—in schools and in different events—our cultural wealth. I recount the history of Québec, the real one, in our oral tradition. I am far from ready to become retired. I still have many years to teach about our peoples. Let us return to our customs, the primary role of the circles. Let's take the speaking feather, one at a time, and listen carefully to what the other says, with our ears and our hearts, in total silence. As taught by our tradition: Observe, listen and act!

Aki Songideye Ikwe
Grandmother Francine Payer

Aki Miskwi Nibi Wabo
Water, The Blood of Mother Earth

Aki Songideye Ikwe nin, Mikinak dodem, Hull Nidonjabà, chi kokum Anishanabe Kwe. My name is Aki Songideye Ikwe, meaning "Strong hearted woman keeper of Mother Earth." Born in Hull, I am Great-Grandmother Anishnabe, from the Turtle Clan. My spiritual journey has significantly expanded following the suicide of my spouse in 1991.

Keeper of ancestral wisdom, I am Grandmother of the Unity Sundance community[30] in Ottawa and of the community, Carrier of the People's Sacred Pipe, the *Poïgan*, Guardian and Carrier of the *Tewehigan* (traditional drum), Seed Keeper and Lodge Keeper of the *Matato* (sweat lodge). I also carry several ceremonies including the Rites of Passage at the Strawberry Moon in June and the Water Ceremony, source of life. Moreover, I facilitate the Full Moon ceremonies and hold women's circles since 14 years. Spokesperson for Mother Earth, I have been sharing my teachings with children in schools for 10 years and I speak to humanity for the well-being of the Seven Generations to come.

---

30. Important ceremony for several Indian nations, which lasts four days during the month of June or July (after the solstice).

For this chapter, I was asked to talk about the blood of our Mother Earth. So, here is what happens during a Water Ceremony: a circle is formed and I begin the smudge. Smudging means burning sage. Using an Eagle Feather, I direct the smoke above each person's head with the sacred grass smoking in a shell. This drives away all negative energy that could have been captured during the day.

There is no particular way to receive the smudging, but according to my tradition, the person initially brings smoke to his eyes in order to release all the things he saw that he should not or did not want to see. He does the same to his ears, to send away all he heard that he should not or did not want to hear, and then to his mouth as the medicine takes all abusive words he might have said and so that those he would pronounce would be beautiful and true. Finally, he brings smudging to his heart in order to listen and talk with it and to open it up to differences. For a woman, it is important to bring the smoke to her belly, where she carries life. Finally, the person turns, and I fumigate his back and under his feet, to have the medicine circulate all around the body.

When I fumigate, I make sure not to touch the hair, because it is sacred. In my nation, we always ask permission before touching someone's hair. Once the smudging is done, I sing, and, as the Water Ceremony is usually done first thing in the morning during a Sunrise Ceremony, I sing The Cherokee Morning Song, to greet Grandfather Sun. Among the Anishnabe, the Sun is our Grandfather and the Moon our Grandmother, while in the Mohawk tradition, the Sun is an elder brother . . .

After, I offer tobacco and water to the Sacred Fire, and I drop some on Mother Earth, to the four directions. I then ask the participants to open their reusable water containers and I invite the women to repeat: "The water that I carry is the blood of Mother Earth." These words change the structure of water.

Indeed, the late Dr. Masaru Emoto did tests before and after the Water Song, at a ceremony held in Washington, a few years ago. The result of the analysis proved without a doubt that this song had changed the structure of the water[31]. So having said the words, the women sing the Water Song in the Algonquin language, facing alternately to the four directions. We begin with the east where the Sun rises and where life begins:

Nibi wabo endayan
Aki misqui nibi wabo

This song, which is more than 300 years old, was sung by our grandmothers for the well-being of water. Only women are invited to sing because *Wabo* means the womb, where we carry our babies. Nevertheless, we invite men in the circle and ask for their support in our battle to save the water, and thereby life.

After singing, water is distributed in the palm of the hand of the participants. Some drink this water; others bring it to their face or their hair . . . Then, in summertime, berries are shared, to honour the precious gifts from Mother Earth. Finally, the tobacco is distributed; each person takes a pinch with the left hand and put his intentions in the tobacco and brings it to his heart. Then we offer it to the water, the fire or Mother Earth, according to circumstances. With the beat of my *tewehigan*, I conclude the ceremony with the Women's Honor Song and the Men's Healing Song, to bring balance and harmony.

Threatened Water

Unfortunately, humans without a doubt threaten water supplies so essential to life. It is estimated that over 70 percent of agricultural land is used for beef production and occupies 30 percent of the planetary surface. To produce 1 kilogram of beef it takes 13,500 litres of water; if you would reduce your meat consumption to 3 days a week instead of 7, you could, all by yourself, preserve up to 40,500 litres of water per week, equivalent to 2,106,000 litres per year.

---

31. Emoto, Masaru. *The Hidden Messages in Water.* Simon & Schuster, 2005.

In the US, 60 million plastic water bottles are consumed each day, 30 million in Europe and over 100 million worldwide. Each year, all around the world, to manufacture only the empty bottles, it takes about 272 billion litres of water and 151 billion litres of petroleum. Consequently, the manufacturing process pollutes significantly by releasing 2.5 million tons of carbon dioxide (CO_2) into the atmosphere. About 86 percent of these bottles are not even recycled, and every second, about 1,500 bottles end up in the ground or the ocean. A thousand years may elapse before decomposition of these is completed.

Access to water is a human right and should under no circumstances be sold. Especially since the bottle, when exposed to sun or freezing, releases dioxin, a carcinogen responsible for breast cancer. And, of course, once at the dump, the bottles release this poison into the environment. This is what we bequeath to our children . . . For all these reasons, water bottles sold in the market are my greatest battle.

Our planet is covered by 70 percent water; 97 percent is salt water and 2.5 percent comes from icebergs. This leaves less than 1 percent for consumption. Every little action helps; from brushing your teeth, to washing the car through the shower . . . Moreover, about 5 minutes in a shower, only consumes 55 to 60 litres of water compared to a bath that takes about 110 liters. Do the math on this one . . .

Our blood contains 82% of water and our brain 85 percent. The six litres of blood circulating in our veins represents a real small inland sea. We can survive for days without food but not without water. A cell does not survive if its environment has dried. However, two-thirds of the water in our body is found in cells.

Because human existence takes place first in women's bodies, and because they are also the ones to provide care for newborns, women are responsible for water. For my part, I take this responsibility very seriously, because water is life.

In my tradition, our ceremonies have to be transmitted in a ceremonial manner[32] in front of the whole community, usually at

---

32. To transmit a ceremony means to pass the responsibility of a ceremony to someone else. The term "ceremonial" means according to rules of usage established for ceremonies.

the Rites of Passage Ceremony for the women during the Strawberry Moon in June. Grandmothers and grandfathers can transmit ceremonies and usually elders can determine who will become an elder. Because a ceremony carrier entails a lot of responsibilities, the ceremony is passed on only when the person is ready. This is done in front of the community, so that those who henceforth carry them are recognized as having the right to do it. Moreover, prior to transmission, the new carrier is prepared by a series of teachings and rituals.

The Water Ceremony is one of the few ceremonies that don't need to be transmitted in a ceremonial way. All women not only have the right, but also the responsibility to do the Water Ceremony. Four people are enough to form a circle: a woman for each direction. So whenever four women gather together, you have a circle and you can hold a ceremony.

A Water Ceremony does not have to be complicated. All we need is a glass of water. We put it on the table, thinking silently about ways to help water in our daily actions, then each in turn we share our thoughts. A discussion may follow and commitments can be made. Then we pronounce these words: "The water that I carry is the blood our Mother Earth." Finally, each takes a sip from the glass . . . and that is a Water Ceremony! What matters here is to raise consciousness about how we use water. She's alive, she deserves love and respect. We should do it for our well-being, our children, our grandchildren and the next Seven Generations.

The Mother Earth Water Walk

In 2011, I walked for the Mother Earth Water Walk from Hawkesbury in eastern Ontario through Sudbury in the north. I traveled more than 500 kilometres, and the journey lasted for almost a month. It all started with a Web publication announcing a walk for the water organized by Grandmother Josephine Mandamine. When I read it, tremors traveled through my whole body and I felt I had to get involved. I immediately sent an email to the coordinator to find out how I could help. She was very happy, because nobody in my area had yet volunteered. At that time, I hadn't even thought of walking; I was more thinking of organizing shelters and fund-raising in my area.

I placed many calls. Everybody was very cooperative. Then the coordinator asked me if I would like to organize the event during the stay of the team in Ottawa. Without hesitation, I said yes and then I prepared and distributed posters. Everything was going well. Friends came from far to be with us. I must say that I received help from my elder, Grandfather William Commanda.

The walk started from the four directions of Turtle Island: East (Maine); South (Mississippi); West (Washington); and North (Manitoba). For each direction, a grandmother was carrying a copper pail along with a GPS system. In each bucket was water from the place of origin of the walker. Some grandmothers were carrying salted water and some others some fresh water. All walkers were reunited in Lake Superior, then converging the salt waters in Bad River, Wisconsin. There were occasions when a little water was added along the way, at places that needed healing[33]. Every evening the water touched down and tobacco was offered, this would also mark the point of departure the next morning.

The journey demanded a lot of determination and courage. Sometimes the grandmothers were walking alone or they suffered bad weather. At one point, walkers from the East group were lost. Indeed, when they came into Québec territory, the authorities forced them to walk onto secondary roads, which completely got them lost . . . I knew I could find them because they were a couple of hours from my home. So I went looking for them and after a few hours of driving and investigation, I finally found them, among other things because I could locate them on the Web, thanks to the GPS.

When I found the walkers, things went very quickly, so I did not have time to think about it. Someone took my car keys, handed me a copper water pail and asked me to walk with Josh, the Golden Eagle Staff Carrier. He told me not to worry, because someone was

---

33. Because the Earth is alive, and like us, she could need healing.

going to bring my car. As we were walking, he was explaining to me to always move forward while carrying the water so that the water never looks back.

I did not expect to start walking that day because I still had to prepare my event in Ottawa, but when we arrived in Grenville[34] where the walkers were sleeping that night, we prepared a cedar foot bath for them and when I saw the bleeding feet of the grandmothers, I realized that I could not abandon them and go home.

Because I knew the road very well, having already lived in this area, the coordinator asked me to be the lead walker up to Highway 17, just outside Pembroke[35]. One morning; when we were close to Highway 148, in Québec, events were telling me to take a different path. There were deer crossing the road as if to prevent us from continuing and eagles flying in circles above our heads. I informed Grandmother Melvina, Grandmother Josephine's sister, that we would take another road. She did not like itinerary changes, especially as our group was already behind schedule.

About half an hour after starting to walk, we smelled a terrible odour, worse than a skunk. For this reason, we offered much tobacco on our way. Another half hour later I realized that we were going in a circle, we were returning to the starting point, and of course as a result, the GPS showed that we had actually turned around. The walkers were panicking . . . I thought I was going to be reprimanded by the coordinator, since this detour took us all morning.

Back to the starting point, Grandfather Gil was waiting for us and expressed that he knew exactly why we had traveled this detour: All residents of this area had no drinking water as all the wells had been contaminated . . . I cried a lot in learning this, and we continued our journey.

I have lived extremely rewarding experiences that have irrevocably changed my life on this trip. I met beautiful people in the heart of the communities we visited. The generosity of people along the way and their love for the water really touched me and gave me hope.

---

34. Municipality located about 100 kilometres from Ottawa.
35. Municipality located about 150 kilometres from Ottawa.

Having lived without running water for nearly eight years, I know the value of the blood of our Mother Earth. Water is worth more than all the gold in the world as without her, life would not exist. This is why I devote myself to raising consciousness about her importance.

Kichi-migwech Kichi-minido minwà nogoding

Great Spirit, thank you for today

Maniteu-Ishkueu
Élyse Vollant

Kepetan
The Path of The Ancestors

I am Maniteu Ishkueu, which means "The woman who visits". I am the mother of eight children and grandmother of seven grandchildren, I am Innu, a *Nitassinan* (territory) Keeper and I live in Mani-Utenam [36].

Kepetan means "the portage paths" that our ancestors used to travel in the territory. These paths still exist today. Moreover, when our ancestors were traveling on rivers, they used poles they left on the shore when they had docked. Many of these poles, which date back thousands of years, are still there marking the passage of many Innu ancestors who walked the *kepetan*.

My grandmother gave birth to my mother in the territory, that is to say, in the woods. When my mother was five or six years old, her family suffered a famine; my grandfather was looking for wild-fowl, but he did not find any. That time was very difficult for them. Harshly marked by this period of famine, my mother decided she would not pass the same experience on to her children, and she chose not to have her family in the territory. With the intention to protect us, she never brought us into the woods.

Nevertheless, I missed the experience of life in the territory. I blamed my parents because they never brought me there. To know

36. Aboriginal reserve (Innu) on the North Shore, to the east of Sept-Iles.

that I was from Innu Nation without being connected to my roots was difficult to accept. Sometimes my parents went into my father's territory, which was not the same as that of my grandfather's. If my father had been alone to decide, he and my mom would have spent all the time in the woods, but my mother did not like to go there at all. So, I swore to myself that I would not deprive my children of that, and at one point I went for two weeks into the territory with them. In the morning, I homeschooled my children, and in the afternoon we made crafts.

My father and my mother had different childhoods. My mother grew up in the territory, and my grandmother taught her children how to make moccasins, tan hides, cook and do many other things. For my father, the family remained in the village and they all went to boarding school, except for him. He told me he went there one day and because he was so turbulent he had been kicked out.

Also, because she wanted to make sure we would not miss anything my mother gave great importance to our studies. So I have a high school diploma, a college certificate in early childhood education and a vocational diploma in carpentry and joinery. But I do not even use them. It gives me the feeling that I have spent time for nothing. At one point, I remember, I was in my carpentry course and I was holding the measuring tape while my teammate noted measurements and I suddenly thought: "But what am I doing here? I should not be here." I knew I had to be somewhere else, but I did not know where at that time.

Later, after giving birth to my youngest daughter, I worked in the daycare where my daughter was going. One day, while I was in charge of the two-year-olds, and my daughter was with the four and five year olds, I passed in front of the room where she was to pick something up, and my daughter asked me: "Do I spend the day with you?" I told her she had to stay with her group, so she added: "I am not supposed to be here. I am supposed to be with my mom." When I came back home, I was really preoccupied. I thought that it was not up to me to take care of the children in my group and that it was not up to someone else to take care of my daughter. All these children had parents and I told myself that it is with them that the children had to be, especially with their mothers.

I finally left the job. My daughter was so happy because we stayed home. Often, when children speak to us, they reveal truths. If we do not try to understand what they mean, we miss something. And it's the same with elders. My parents educated us to respect them: "When an elder enters the room, get up and give him or her your place". There are always teachings that come through the elders. This is also what I have taught my children. Moreover, it seems that when an elder dies, he feels distraught as he is not certain that someone else will continue to take care of our Mother Earth in turn.

A lot of people believe that with ancestors in some Native nations, such as the Algonquins, it was the men who led, but I don't think so. For example, when the family was moving on its territory, the woman decided when it was time to stop, because she had to feed the children. If the man had been alone, or if he had been with other men, they would have continued; but women, because of the children, decided when the group should stop.

My people have walked a lot through the *kepetan*, and we still walk a lot today: not because we have to move, but to mobilize people and demonstrate our solidarity with one another.

This spring, with my son, Emery, my brother Mohawk, Stuart, and his son, Ranenhahawi, I walked for a month and a half, from Revelstoke in British Columbia to Ottawa[37]. We visited our brothers and sisters of different territories, transmitting the message that it is urgent, for the well being of our Mother Earth and the life she carries, that we bring back the power to our Mothers.

I walked for the 1,200 missing and murdered Native women over the past 30 years. I walked for their parents and friends. I walked for the women to regain the place that belongs to them. I walked for the mothers to recover their power, so that our communities could again find their identity. I walked for the government

---

37. Over 3,700 kilometres separate Revelstoke from Ottawa (a part of this trip was traveled by car).

to put an end to the genocide of First Nations Peoples. I walked for the protection of our Mother Earth.

In the different territories we visited, we were invited to radio shows to talk about our work. Also, new friendships were established. We met residential school[38] survivors, and I was happy to find that they still live their spirituality according to their traditions, despite their experiences. Moreover, we were housed and fed by very friendly people who often offered us presents. I sometimes had my heart torn when it was time to hit the road again. Today when I look back, I thank our Mother Earth for having guided us toward good people.

During the walk, I proudly carried the Innu flag that represents us, but the one day that my Mohawk brothers could not walk because of blisters, I walked alone while carrying the Mohawk flag, and I felt happy because of that solidarity. Obviously we've had difficult days. For example, we had to face the snow or the slopes on the roads. Moreover, we missed our loved ones; I left my husband, my other children and my grandchildren in Québec. Emery has a three-year-old daughter and a couple of two-year-old twins, while Stuart is the father of a second son who is 16 years old.

Through walking, I was completely shocked to see whole territories emptied of the trees that populated them. I did not understand how people without remorse and without concern for future generations could do that. I cried a lot. I also prayed to our Mother Earth, asking her to open our eyes to the evil that we are imposing upon her. I asked her to wake the bear who had hibernated, but never woke up. I asked her to make us aware of the pain she suffered so all those who carry the Good Spirit become her guardians.

At one point, we walked into a community where we met a 28-year-old man. He explained to us that in his community there are gangs that clash. Members of these groups fight between cousins and even between brothers. The band council[39] does not stop

---

38. See note 20, page 86.
39. See note 4, page 22.

them because the chief of the council himself is part of a gang. I was sad to see how some communities may have lost their path. Nevertheless, I found the courage to move forward relentlessly in this expedition, encouraged by Nutaui, my late father, my hero. My father had always protected our Mother Earth. He died three years ago, but I know he always accompanies me when I walk. I also know that we were accompanied by the Good Spirit and the spirit of the Great Eagle.

The fact of crossing Anglophone territories and not to speak English has never been a barrier for me, even if my Mohawk brothers who walked with us only speak English. We came to communicate beyond words. Of course, Emery speaks some English and served as interpreter when necessary, but we all walked together during this month and a half with the same goal, without needing to talk a lot to understand one another.

Besides, I experienced a great transformation, thanks to Stuart. One day, long ago before this walk, he said: "How can you defend the Earth? You are not even connected to your identity." Indeed, my family had been converted to the Catholic religion and I grew up with that. But my identity is Innu. The Catholic Church is not part of my identity. Stuart told me that if I really wanted to reconnect with the Earth, I had to first come back to who I really am. For me it was like a slap that woke me up. It is certain that I did not come back to my identity in one day. I needed time.

Several people in my community claim to be spiritual and traditional, but they are confused. For example, during ceremonies, at some point, the question of Jesus would come up. Because it concerned me, I talked about it with my father. He always left us free to choose the way we live, but he said: "You cannot follow two paths. If you have two canoes and you have a foot in each, you'll end up falling into the water . . . "

One day in 2012, I participated in a blockade against Hydro Québec. Even after two referendums in our community where the answer was *no*, Hydro Québec did not take into account the decision of my people and continued its work, which showed a great lack of respect for us[40]. However, since the band council supported the blockade, we felt stronger, and it gave us the courage to close the road. Unfortunately, two days after the beginning of the blockade, the band council recanted because it accepted the financial compensation offered by Hydro-Québec. In contrast, the council could not immediately receive the money because a group of women, including myself, continued to block the road. Our territory was more important than Hydro Québec's money. We (the women) refused to give up, because we wanted to protect the heritage of future generations.

We continued to block the road, searching inside all the trucks coming, and we demanded that all Hydro-Québec vehicles turn back. The pressure we were under was great. Over a 1000 workers could not work because we were the blocking the way. On the Friday, that is to say the fifth day of blockade, we were arrested and imprisoned by the authorities: twelve women and one man. That day, before going to the front, I remember I was in the car with my dad and I said: "But what should I do? The cause is dear to my heart. Since Monday I have been here and I block the path, but there are almost no more women." He looked at me without saying a word. He could not decide for me. Then the police came and, in solidarity, I got out of the car to reach the front.

When we were released, we were not allowed to talk among ourselves, but this was ridiculous because in the group, there were a woman and her daughter who were living in the same house. I do not know if it was to influence the band council, as a third referendum was coming, but nobody got a criminal record through this event.

Some people in the territory had installed a *shaputuan*, meaning "big tent", so that we could gather and have speaking circles in order to find solutions. We thought that it was necessary that when

---

40. In March 2012, some members of the community, most of whom were women, blocked highway 138, because Hydro-Québec proceeded with imposing a high voltage electrical transmission line on the territory, although the community had refused it in two referendums.

we say *No*, it is a clear and respected *No*. We met people from many communities who traveled to come and help us: Natashquan, Mingan, La Romaine and others. Also, this is how I met people of the Traditional Council of Kahnawake.

During the same period, an official opening of the camp took place. At this moment, something happened that shook me up. I was in the *shaputuan*, where the floor was covered with fir branches, and an elder struck the *teueikan*, which means "drum." Then I started to cry because I felt at the same time a vibration that traveled from the ground and went through my whole being. I was feeling in my body what our Mother Earth felt.

Some time after these events, under the sound of *teueikan*, we started walking from the First Nations camp of Mani-Utenam, to get to Montréal to celebrate Earth Day. Initially, we were 14 women and 2 drivers for the vehicles that were following us. It was a relay walk: We formed teams of two and each team walked five kilometers. We were showing our disagreement with Plan Nord[41]. We want our rights to be recognized, especially for future generations. It is also at the end of this walk that I participated in my first Full Moon Ceremony at Kahnawake.

After that, I often returned to visit the people of the Longhouse, and when it was time to hit the road, the elder always told me: "Go with what you feel. If the ceremonies were lost in your community, do your ceremonies with what you feel." I learn so much every time I come to Kahnawake, but I do not reproduce their ceremonies, because I think it's important for me to do it with my own identity: I am not Mohawk, I am an Innu woman.

When our Mother Earth suffers violence, the mothers feel it, because they give life like she does. Mothers must reconnect to the Earth to really understand and feel who they must defend. When a woman reclaims her identity, her partner feels she is well, also her children and everyone around, so automatically, everyone is influenced by this woman.

---

41. Immense exploitation project of natural resources (the vital forces of the Earth) in the northern regions of the province of Québec, where Native people live.

Definitely, power has to be brought back to women, from the youngest child to the oldest grandmother. This is how we reclaim our identity, which is also that of our ancestors. By doing so, we will reclaim our ceremonies, our songs and our language. Only in this way, will we become true guardians of our Mother Earth, as were our ancestors.

Tin Ifsen

Farida Zerar

Takvaylit Ghur Warraw N Tmurt
A Kabyle Woman in Native Land

I am Tin Ifsen, which means "The blossomed." I am the daughter of Wezna Bouaoudand Acur Zerar; I am the granddaughter of Djouher Chemlal and Ali Buaud, my maternal grandparents. I am also the granddaughter of Tasadit Fahem and Hocine Serer, my paternal grandparents; these are women and men I honour.

Visiting the Mohawk territory, I present myself as a humble guest to *Kanienke'ha'ka*, their ancestors and guardian spirits of their land. I do so with respect and gratitude and I honour them. I thank them for welcoming me to the Longhouse. I wish that our Mother Earth may guide my words and that our exchange participates in taking care of her and in spreading peace and friendship between us and our children, for us and for future generations.

I come from *Tamurt n Iqvayliyen*: meaning "the Kabyle Country." I have lived in Québec for the past 20 years: a part of the world that I cherish. Before I left Kabylia, my father advised me to offer myself to the service of my host society, as we have been serving our original one. I learned that understanding the other is to understand a part of oneself, because *nothing that is human can be alien to me*. So sometimes I present myself as *kabycoise*.

Kabylie is located northeast of Algeria, in North Africa. The Kabyle people form one of the Amazigh (Berber) indigenous nations that historically, geographically and culturally, have populated Tamazgha (Berber territory) for millennia. Among the countries that make up this vast area are the North African countries: Algeria, Morocco, Tunisia, Libya and Mauritania. The word "Africa" itself comes from the Kabyle term *tafarka*, which means "land ownership." The *imazighen* term means "free men and women those who inhabit Tamazgha."

I was born in Algiers, the capital of Algeria, and spent a part of my youth there. Though I spent much of my life in Algiers, I have no meaningful recollection of it. It's as if I had not lived there. Nevertheless, the brightest memories of my childhood come from my village in Kabylia during the school holidays. When I close my eyes, I see the snowy Djurdjura, our sacred mountain. I can still see its peaks and houses clinging to the sides of the hills in the morning mist. I hear the rain drumming on the roof of our house and I smell the wood burning in the fireplace. There, time stands still, my soul settles, I'm home.

Until the age of six, I spoke only Kabyle, because my mother speaks neither Arabic nor French. However, the men in my family spoke Kabyle and French perfectly. The school was, therefore, a shock: The instruction was in Arabic, a language foreign to me. Moreover, Arabic and French are the languages of our colonizers. Because my mother did not speak them, she was socially considered illiterate. Arabic was imposed to the detriment of indigenous languages while French was our bulwark against the Arabic language that was presented as the sacred language of the Koran.

Even if at school I did not understand what I was told, I felt hostility and mockery toward me. It was only some years later that I realized that people treated us (the Kabyle) as wild Indians and considered our language gibberish or wild English. It must be said that many American westerns were broadcast on the single Algerian television channel in the '70s and haunted the popular imagination. Fellag, a Kabyle[42], commented on the phe-

---

42. He was the interpreter of M. Lazhar, in the movie of the same name, produced by the Québécois, Philippe Falardeau.

nomenon of the hatred of the Kabyle: "What they did not know was that they were all Kabyle!" Indeed, a few years later, my father taught me that Algeria, which is called an Arab country, is not Arab, and Islam has not always been the religion of the Tamazgha countries.

It was after one of the most violent conquests of Algeria that the Arabic language and Islam entered it. The invasion of Algeria began as early as 647, but our ancestors resisted the repeated attacks until 701. Among them was Queen Dyhia, whom the Arabs nicknamed *Kahina*, meaning "witch." They captured and beheaded her. Then, in 1530, Algeria fell under Turkish rule within the Muslim Ottoman Empire that perpetuated the caliphate. Only Kabylia escaped this and has kept its own social and political organization intact.

The French arrived in 1830, and Algiers was taken in a few days, but it was only in 1857 that French soldiers managed to penetrate Kabyle territory. Among those who opposed them, a woman, Fadma N'Sumer, organized the resistance and mobilized the Kabyle population against the French General, Randon, who nicknamed her "the Joan Arc of Djurdjura." She died in captivity at the age of 33.

My father took part in this war. In 1954, he left his native village, leaving behind my mother and my brothers who were born before 1954. He returned in 1962, the year of Independence. The village welcomed him as a hero, but my brothers, who had grown up without him, did not recognize him. I was born a year after this reunion.

As a child, I knew nothing of this reality and as our culture and our language were valorized in my family, I was never ashamed of who I am. So I learned Arabic and French without difficulty while growing up in the enchanted world of Yemma, meaning "Mom" in Kabyle). She taught me that the ancestral land, my Kabylia, is sacred. She taught me that there is the visible world and the invisible world, the latter being populated by guardian spirits. Every house, every place has its own guardian spirit and energy. I remember seeing women greeting the places they visited by doing a circular motion of the hand and then kissing it, saying: "With respect, Oh guardian of these places!"

There is a threshold between the visible and the invisible that we cannot cross in any way. According to Kabyle spirituality, poets, madmen, sages, mystics, scholars and people with tragic and exceptional destinies are among those who cross this threshold, and we respect them. They could be men or women, and could come back stronger or weaker from these trips; they nevertheless have something to teach us about ourselves and they can make us aware of other dimensions. They can be spiritual guides, but they never impose themselves because everyone is responsible for his or her own spiritual evolution.

We have no word for religion, and spirituality is lived in communion with nature. We have the custom of celebrating all seasons, but the spring is the one that I prefer: *tafsut*, in the Kabyle language. I was 10 when I took part in it. Dressed for the occasion, adults and children, we went out into the fields. We picked flowers and we crushed the petals in our hands to coat our faces with their sap. We danced, sang and ate together. It was wonderful! On the way back, I saw my mother put couscous grains near the entrance of an anthill. She explained that she had always seen her mother feed the ants, because it is good for the Earth. So, I'm always a little annoyed when I kill an ant.

After that my mother made a detour to the fountain to carry out the ritual of purification. It consists simply of refreshing the face and hands with the intention of purifying all that can be harmful for us. She then left bread in a clean bag as an offering. The passerby who finds and picks it up eats the bread, so he or she also participates in the healing ritual.

At night we would go out to contemplate the Moon. In the silence of the Kabylia sky full of stars, I felt I was in communion with the Universe. I was small, but was in connection with a whole of which I was a part. I bathed in bliss and love. I began to understand what my mother would often repeat: "It is better to meditate on the mystery of creation than to be locked in a religious dogma."

It is this sacred space that, for me, was ransacked on April 20, 1980. On the occasion of the Spring Festival, students from the University of Tizi-Ouzou, the main city of Kabylia, had organized a conference on Amazigh poetry with Mouloud Mammeri, a Kabyle writer and linguist. The conference was banned, and students demonstrated in the streets of Tizi-Ouzou. They were suppressed in blood and several were imprisoned. I was in Algiers when these events took place. In solidarity, I wore the Kabyle scarf for several days, adorned with a pin that is worn for special occasions. Since *Tafsut imazighen*, the Berber Spring is commemorated in Kabylia and worldwide by the Kabyle diaspora.

Some years after the bloody Berber Spring, I returned to live in Kabylia and to spend time in my grandparents' house: *tazekka*, meaning "the great Kabyle house". In my grandfather's time, it was always crowded. In addition to hosting guests among friends and relatives, they also welcomed *inebgawen n rabbi*. This is how we call all those who are in need. They are *ddow lanaya*, that is to say, under the protection of the village, a family or a clan. I remember the time when my cousins and I would gather at my grandparents' place. We slept side by side and sometimes there were so many of us that, when one of us wanted to turn over, we all had to turn over.

Unfortunately, violence did not end on April 20, 1980. In 1988, an Algerian gendarme shot at close range our poet and singer Lounes Matoub who was committed to the defence of our identity and the liberation of Algeria dominated by Arab-Muslim ideology. He did not die that day. Then in 1994, Muslim fundamentalists kidnapped him but released him under pressure from the Kabyle people.

By the '90s, the violence got worse: Many massacres, slaughters, and rapes occurred. The Algerian elite, including several Kabyles, was the target of Muslim fundamentalists. In 1998, Lounes Matoub was finally murdered on a road in Kabylia. I was in Montréal when I heard the news of his death. I joined hundreds of Kabyles who marched in the streets of Montréal and I shouted with them: "Correct history: Algeria is not Arab!" This murder is part of the terror and violence that strikes my people with its most powerful symbols, but I was far from suspecting that this terror was to cross the borders of my country and to be directed at symbols like Theo Van Gogh or *Charlie Hebdo*.

Lounes Matoub is buried at his home. According to the Kabyle tradition, those who are buried at their home died of an unpunished murder, of which we must remember. His grave is a place of pilgrimage. In the same vein, on April 20, 2001, over 100 Kabyles were arbitrarily killed and more than 5,000 were seriously injured in Kabylia. All these crimes remain unpunished to this day.

Algerian Muslim fundamentalists raped our women, the women of their own people, as the Arab and Turkish conquerors had done before them, in the name of an Islam that was imposed by violence and is maintained through terror. My parents taught me to cry for those executioners, as they are part of the children of Algeria, who were cut off from the spiritual strength of their ancestral Amazigh roots, and they suffered identity alienation. They have internalized contempt, hatred and shame of themselves, thereby imitating those who colonized them. Are they trying to make sense of the violence that inhabits them? I admire the young Kabyles who wrote "Liberty" with their own blood before dying under fire from Arab and Muslim fundamentalists, including all those in Algeria and elsewhere who stand up to barbarism.

After the death of my grandparents, an aunt who was a widow moved into their house. Thanks to her, our family house kept its tradition of welcoming people: It became a place where women of my village gathered in a circle and exchanged views on anything and everything. How many times did I fall asleep to the sound of their voices, lying on the floor, my head on my mother's knees. I still hear one of them, an elder, talking about her faith. For this generation, the experience of the sacred is in the order of spiritual intimacy that is indecent to exhibit in a conspicuous manner. According to us, spirituality means freedom of conscience for each one.

Honouring our ancestors is essential, since they have walked the path of life before us. We inherit the consequences of their actions, good or bad and, combined with the consequences of our own actions, we transmit those in turn to our children. Thus, the best way to protect our offspring from suffering is to prevent them from carrying the weight of our actions.

Death and life are two sides of the same coin; those who die are part of the invisible world. However, the dead remain among the dead and the living among the living. We must not hold on to those who die by feeling too much sadness or pain. I learned this the hard way when, a few days after his funeral, I tried to contact my brother, Amazuz Rachid, who was murdered by Islamists. I was surprised when my father told me that Amazuz had come to visit him in his dream and told him he needed to find peace. I broke the rules through ignorance. Moreover, one of the women of the village was the "night messenger" for another brother I lost. That woman saw him in a dream, at the edge of a small tomb, holding a little girl in his arms. He did not know who she was. We later discovered that she was a cousin whose tomb did not have a name.

I love the festive side of our funeral rituals. With the help of their families, mourners prepare a meal for the whole village. Several days following the death, it is the village that feeds them. The deceased person spends the night at home where a vigil is organized. The men sing throughout the night, and in the morning the women take over. These songs express an ancient poetry and help to relieve the pain of loss.

What fascinates me is the simplicity with which the profane and the sacred spaces coexist in everyday life. I remember the death of one of my aunts. A few moments before she died, she calmly pointed to the corner of the room. We saw nothing, but she told us that there was a woman, and that was death that came to fetch her. A few days later, a large butterfly was flying around above the bed where my aunt passed away. I heard my cousin shout to her children: "Do not touch the butterfly; it is the soul of your aunt that says goodbye." In Kabyle culture, butterflies symbolize the souls of the dead.

For us, nature is a sacred temple and the body of the woman, as the image of our Mother Earth, is honoured. Sexuality is experienced in cosmic connection to the sacred nature and the language of love is inspired from it. For example, one said about a virgin that she is a land that has never been ploughed, and about a man who has erection problems that life has left him. With us, it is men who sing the freedom, beauty and dignity of women. Man owes respect and protection to the woman, but both are at the service of life and can give spiritual guidance. My mother taught me to love and respect men, because without them our homes and villages would be empty and dull. My father taught me that as a woman I carry a great power and I am valuable. He also taught me that my identity might be bruised, but it is not murderous. He made me a free woman.

My grandfather's house is now empty. All the generations of men and women who lit it up have traveled to the other side. I wait for my time to join them. I thank the Kabyle mountain dwellers who still bear the burden of memory. They allowed me to connect with the strength of my roots and taught me to respect the otherness.

I have spoken. I have told my truth.

HO[43]!

---

43. Among Aboriginal people in a speaking circle, *Ho!* means "I have spoken."

Edith Mora Castelán

Ba'dudxaapa'caxana
Woman Giving Birth

I was born in what is now known as Mexico City, the former territory of Tenochtitlan, the Mexica-Aztec territory. My parents, both immigrants from within the country, settled in the suburbs. When I was a little girl, I often visited my grandmother who taught me to cook and to prepare drinks just as she did in her native village, in the mountains, on the banks of a river, on the Isthmus of Tehuantepec, Oaxaca. She told me stories, life lessons which I guess she was hoping that I could remember in the future. She loved reading after eating, lying down to rest with her little book falling from her hands once her eyes closed. I found it amusing to imitate her and, when she fell asleep, I gazed upon her; she was so beautiful, so strong.

As a teenager, I saw fields and hills filled with cows and grass quickly transform into a series of track homes. I also saw the first shopping centers pop up in the area, as well as the first fast-food chains. At the time, I did not realize how lucky I was to have a mother waiting for me after school with a good meal, ready to help me with my homework. I also had a father who worked hard to provide my mother and me with everything we needed. My parents gave me the best of themselves: love, protection and opportunities. With their support, and because I loved languages, I learned English and French, and I was also able to work and study. Then life took me to Montréal, a place I fell deeply in love with (it was summer, of course). Soon after, I went back there to continue my studies.

Far from my usual settings and close to a new way of seeing the world, I began to get interested in environmental issues, indigenous peoples and problems of injustice. When I returned to Mexico, I was not the same, and I quickly decided to leave for Québec, thinking it was a place where I could find myself. However, before I returned, I discovered Malinalco, a town southwest of Mexico City, where in the past, the ancient Tenochtitlan people honoured the Jaguar and Eagle Warriors, protectors of the balance of our Mother Earth, in her nocturnal and diurnal appearances.

Returning to Montréal, I was welcomed by my new points of reference: my friends. They helped me to move forward and establish myself, but mostly to get acquainted with the *Kanienke'ha'ka* Traditional Council from Kahnawake. The day I arrived, Montrealers walked the streets, advocating for the adoption of the charter of Indigenous Peoples. I was in favor of the Charter too, until I understood what it really was. At that point, I did not imagine that this would lead me back to my original identity.

Some perceive the Charter of Indigenous Peoples to be a good thing; however, it is perhaps the fatal blow of a genocidal process against original peoples.

First, the word "development" has an economic meaning outcome of colonialist thinking that treats our Mother Earth as a resource to be exploited. But indigenous peoples, from their original identity, understand and protect the Earth, because they know what she represents: the one that gives us life and everything we need to stay alive. The fact that the declaration grants the First Nations peoples the right to development contradicts the very essence of native peoples, especially as it perverts their identity.

Second, Native peoples have their own way to govern themselves and make decisions that relies on a council process to obtain a consensus. The declaration instead sets out a consultative approach for any project (such as mines and dams) being imposed on Native land. However, this consultation comes with a questionnaire designed to persuade native communities to accept a pre-approved vision of the project (not to mention the non-official methods that use threats and even violence). Moreover, such consultation legitimizes an electoral system that not only protects corrupt lobbying but goes against the traditional governing process of Native peoples: the Council. If the purpose of the charter was really to restore what has been taken from the Native communities, it would give them the means to rebuild their identity (education, social constitution, Earth's protection) instead of continuing to impose approaches that greenlight projects that destroy the health of Earth and its population.

Third, how can we consider fair the excuses of an authority that continues to act the same way? Excuses are invalid and become a form of manipulation, even violence. If one breaks something, would one not be obliged to fix it? The fabric of indigenous peoples who had always put women at the centre of life is torn apart. What do the systems, the governments responsible for repairing this, do? This is exactly where the current challenge is.

With the *Kanienke'ha'ka* Traditional Council of Kahnawake, I experienced my first Thanksgiving Ceremony dedicated to Maple Water, medicine of our Mother Earth, just when the snows begin to melt in early spring. Then there was the Celebration of the Summer Solstice, and in conjunction with southern friends (Chile, Ecuador, etc.) we performed a Ceremony of the Eagle and Condor to unite the peoples of the South and North. I also experienced other Thanksgiving Ceremonies throughout the year; ceremonies that bind us to what our Mother gives us (*tionkhiia:wis*) through the seasons, during her journey around the Sun, along the 13 lunations. This is what was missing in my life—*gratitude*—and I found it back there.

Motivated by the desire to learn about my native roots, I began to regularly participate in the Council activities. So, we presented a play about residential schools[44]; I took part in Full Moon Ceremonies organized in town and in women circles; in planting

---

44. See note 2, page 89.

and cultivating a traditional garden at the Longhouse where we are growing the Three Sisters (Corn, Bean and Squash); as well as in Native culture and spirituality workshops for children; in conferences and panels about environment where I act especially as interpreter from French or Spanish to English for Council members who speak English. Above all, with the Council, I met several great people from different backgrounds, other countries and other cultures, with whom we have built international relations. It's wonderful when Native peoples meet and find their similarities, confirming that we come from the same place: our Mother Earth. One of the most recent meetings was with the indigenous people of Kabylie, now called Algeria, whose women are strong and deep-rooted. Then finally, my involvement has led the Council to place me under the protection of the Wolf Clan.

Thanks to my relation with the Traditional Council, I am now proud of my indigenous origins from the Zapotec nation, which makes me a Zapotec too since in matrilinearity we follow our mother's bloodline to identify ourselves and my blood line is Zapotec. Before, I was unaware of this origin because my ancestors had to hide our original identity not to be discriminated against in a mixed Mexico where the bloodline comes from the father (it was not like this before) and where language and the imposed new identity devalues all others.

When we are in council, the Good Mind (the goal of working together to solve an issue) leads us to find rallying points. To reach an agreement, the council process allows everyone to express themselves. The differences are discussed until they are erased. The idea is not to make concessions as if we were in negotiations with winners and losers as a result. Rather, it is to arrive at a set of reasoning in which we can distinguish what is right from what is not, creating from many voices one consensus voice. The best way to change or adopt a behaviour is not by obedience, but because it becomes a part of us.

In council, women have their own voices, separate from that of men, which reproduces the Creation (the seed is female first, and then it may be appointed male). First, women gather, express themselves and come to a consensus. Second, the result of this consensus is presented to men who repeat the same process. And finally, the subject is discussed in Great Council. Through this process, everyone is included and has an equal opportunity to express themselves within the different levels of representativeness, in order to solve a problem. Above all, everyone takes part in the decision making, eliminating the democratic loophole that generates overwhelming majorities and frustrated minorities. The Council, a human process that comes from Creation, allows for being aware of the *onkwaneristha* by which we live: We are bound to the Earth and we make decisions for the purpose of her welfare, which is also ours.

Onkwaneristha[45]
The Umbilical Cord

Forced to run without taking the time to look at where we are going, we may lose the magic of life, and no longer understand it. This magic is so simple. It hides itself like the beauty of a seed (*kahna*) under the ground, ready to sprout without having given its very first leaves. It is there, even if we do not see it, and yet it is full of life.

The seed of each human life is the constant repetition of Creation itself and it divides itself to give shape to life. In the womb, early in the gestation-creation process, the seed is female. It will become male only later, if selected as such. But this seed does not grow by itself, it feeds through the umbilical cord that attaches directly to the mother, the one who will feed and provide until the completeness of the growth period, as in a garden where the seeds do not grow by themselves, but through the combining with water, land, sun and shade.

When women are at peace, when they enjoy unrestricted mobility in which they can have control of their lives, they acquire an unparalleled solidity which they transfer to their

---

45. The title of the chapter is in Zapotec, while the subtitles are in mohawk.

children. Most of the time, this strength is transmitted by the environment through the love of others, through other women of the family, and through the land of the ancestors. If a woman is peaceful during the process of gestation-creation of a new life, she bequeaths this peace to her child from the very beginning and she will continue after the birth, with the support of the entourage.

At the end of the growth period, the umbilical cord should be cut off physically, but the link between mother and child will last forever. Invisible once the baby is born, it is his strongest link.

What happens then when a woman experiences shortage, war, fear, abuse, suffering, stress, anger, denial, when she does not remember where she comes from?

Iakon:kwe Karonhiakeh:son, Ionkhisotha Ahsonthennekha Karahkwa tanon Ionkhi'nistenh:a Ohontsa
Sky Woman, Our Grandmother Moon, and Our Mother Earth

Like every child, humanity was born of a mother: our Mother Earth. And for there to be life, our Grandmother Moon started spinning around the Earth by creating a connection from one gravity point to another, invisibly linking the Moon to the Earth, like an umbilical cord. It is for this reason that the Moon is our grandmother. However, for the Earth and Moon to exist, Sky Woman, the first being, had to gather cosmic dust while dropping slowly, accumulating particles to create the Moon and the Earth.

When our Grandmother Moon began to turn around our Mother Earth, she completed 13 laps while Mother Earth went through a complete revolution around the Sun. That's when Sky Woman landed on the back of the Turtle (Mother Earth), and she started to dance around her creating the 13 squares on the back of the Turtle equivalent to 13 moons included in a solar cycle which correspond to the 13 moons that women experience in their bodies throughout a solar cycle. Thus, there is a strong invisible but undeniable link between Sky Woman, Grandmother Moon, Mother Earth, and all women related to them and sharing the same role: Creation.

Kasentsatshera Konnonkwe
The Power of Women Today

Being a woman today is a challenge. We face several obstacles that may distract us from our femininity. First, babies are born most of the time in cold hospitals, away from grandmothers' hands who should receive the small newborns. Then, the mothers are often forced to send their children to daycare where they will learn, if they succeed, to excel in a system based on performance, kept away from the love and maternal protection of their mother who should be present to guide and teach them how to behave in life. Furthermore, the mother's task is more complicated when she is single and cannot count on the support of her own mother, her sisters and her grandmother to help with the education of her children, since they need other reference points besides their mothers, daycare educators or teachers. All children, but especially boys, need to hear and meet several female voices, which could also prevent many cases of Oedipus complex.

The *onkwanerista*, our umbilical cord, disappears when we, women, do not convey our love for Creation, when we forget the 13 moons of the year, when we do not learn to appreciate our lunar month period and when we are taught to perform and compete against others, both men and women. In this context, we are unable to learn the power of women.

Of course, women live with a broken heart. It is broken by so much destruction and violence, by years of lack of respect from men who do not recognize the key role of women within Creation. Yet, it is women who are the pillars of families, of communities and of societies, still these societies dare to call women (life givers) minorities. What happens if the majority is wrong? After so many years of being imposed on and of being pulled apart, women today have two major challenges: not to perpetuate what is imposed on them, and to trust other women.

First, it is not because the men have snatched the power from women and torn their femininity, leading humanity to an imbalance, that women should take revenge. A woman cannot be equal to a man. How could she, if she is the one who transmits life to him? Instead, the woman may recognize her identity without taking back by force what was stolen from her; she would then be able to find, with the help of other women, the power of her femininity.

For a long time, women have been forced to compete with each other rather than to help each other, to collaborate. In this context, mutual trust has become difficult to obtain. Moreover, self-recognition depends on recognition and concern for each other, and on working with others, all of which leads to communication, listening, patience, openness, laughter, love, sharing, joy, music and so on. All this is possible without claiming that one woman is better than the other but by being aware that we are all different, and, in our uniqueness, together, we find strength. To get there, it is necessary for men to support women in this process, so that they are encouraged. Once men see and experience this magic with women, they will want to protect it and to make the feeling last. And for that, both women and men need to focus their efforts in order to be aware of their respective roles and to help each other discover that they are involved in the process of exploring matrilineality: the balance between them.

In the *Kanienke'ha'ka* Creation story, and also in the Mayan one, there are twins. These are the first sons of our Mother Earth, the guarantors of balance. According to the Mohawk Creation Story, the first one was born in a natural way, but the mother died giving birth to the second one. As a result, this son always believed that he killed his mother. His guilt made him nasty to the point that he began to destroy Creation. But in reality he did not kill his mother; she gave her life for him. When he understands this, he feels so grateful that he begins to work in balance with his twin brother. The Twins are inside of us, and we can get them to work together, in balance once again.

 Edith Mora Castelán

Ahsen Kontateken:en
The Three Sisters

The story of the Three Sisters is something that I learned in the Longhouse from other women. This is not something that I invented or that I came up with. And those women got that knowledge from the women that were there before them. It is something that has been passed down by the women of the house throughout time.

The *Kanienke'ha'ka* people say that they would not have the matrilineal authority and the Great Law of Peace constitution without corn. It is corn that has allowed them to establish and develop the political constitution that is linked to the spiritual one.

Corn comes from the south, somewhere in Central America or South America. Many countries would claim it comes from there, but anyway this is not the point. It grew from the ground somewhere and it came to other people with the knowledge of how to take care of it, because Corn is one of the plants that needs help to grow.

Corn is the eldest of the Three Sisters. She was born of the breast of our Mother Earth, because when the plant starts to grow a little bit tall, she needs help to be propped up. Indeed, when there is rain or wind, she might fall down and break from the bottom, close to the ground. In order to prevent this from happening, people gather and grab earth and pat it around Corn to try to make a little mountain around her, to prop her up. That little mountain around her is like the breast a baby drinks milk from; it is like our Mother Earth's breast.

Moreover, when Corn comes out of the stalk, the first thing we see is hair. It brings to mind the labour of the woman giving birth; it is like the head of the baby that we see coming out. And when the corn is tender, and almost ready to be harvested, if we squeeze a raw kernel, we will see white liquid that looks like milk, the sustenance of any baby.

Bean is the second of the Three Sisters. There are many varieties of beans, the bush bean that grows near the ground and the pole bean which is the one we have at the Longhouse. She grows around a pole, so she climbs up in the counter clockwise direction. One day at the Longhouse, somebody wanted to help Bean grow, so he wrapped her up around a pole, but he did so in a clockwise direction. Bean unwrapped and then rewrapped herself around in a counter clockwise way. That means the energy of the Earth goes like that: in a counter clockwise direction (no wonder why we feel we are running when we follow the clock, going against our Mother Earth's vital force!)

When Bean is already mature, she looks like the fingers of the hand. That is why it is like the caress of our Mother Earth, because a newborn baby needs sustenance, but also the love of its mom. So if the baby is crying, the surest thing that will sooth it are the caresses of the mother.

Finally, Squash, the youngest of the Sisters, represents the belly button. If we look at her, the way she grows, the main cord will go further away, exactly like an umbilical cord when the baby is growing in the womb of its mother. Moreover, the baby cannot grow if there is no umbilical cord. And at the end of the pregnancy, the belly of the mother looks like a big squash, which represents the baby.

Only the female flower grows with the little baby squash in it, so only the female one gives life. Even if Squash grows away, she always keeps connected to the centre. And she has some kind of vines to be able to grab onto the plants or grass that she will find on her way in order to continue to grow, to reach out to life. So life holds onto life.

Corn, Bean and Squash grow together and help each other. That is why they are called the Three Sisters. Corn stands up, Bean will climb around her, and Squash has little thorns that protect her sisters from predators. This is an inspiring figure of how women can be: like sisters helping each other to grow.

One story says that at the time the nomad peoples were walking to get food, a moment came where it was very hard for all of them to continue. The women turned around and saw the elders and the kids completely tired and having problems walking, so they told the men: "We cannot continue like this. Some are tired and we need to stop. Go and hunt, we are going to stay here and we will wait for you." The men, who were in a rush to follow the animals, left.

After a very long time, when the men came back, they found a clearing in the woods where there were little houses, and a fire was burning. There were laughter and happiness, kids were playing around, and elders were resting and teaching the kids how to do things. There was a garden where the women were cultivating some plants: Corn, Bean and Squash that allowed them to settle down, and to take care of the people who needed care. At this point, the men knew that they could not do whatever they wanted, because it was the women's houses, the women's place, and they had to respect it. This is how they all kept the balance.

Today, the love of our mothers is missing. The heart of women must heal. When women recognize themselves, when they recover their power, everything becomes possible.

Ie'ne:kwen'sinekens
Full Moon

The Beating Heart
of Our Mother Earth

When I heard the Moon Teaching for the first time,
I understood nothing. The second time, I began to grasp
the fundamentals.
The third time I understood, but I would not have been able
to explain it. I was finally able to write it after hearing
it several times.
The oral tradition of Native peoples is heard by all repeatedly
from an early age. This is how they integrate and are able to
transmit it in their turn.
Because it is oral tradition that has never been published before,
some of the following chapters may require more than one
reading to grasp their essence.

GUYLAINE CLICHE

 Katsitenserio

Stuart Myiow Junior

Ieronhiakaiehronon
Sky Woman

U sually, the only time the Creation story is spoken properly is within a Law Recital through oral tradition, so it is very hard to transfer it to a book the way we are doing here. Nevertheless, certain details can be addressed.

It may be hard to imagine the very beginning of the Creation because when we talk about the beginning, we talk about prior to there being anything: no physical matter, nothing to imagine, nothing to dream, nothing to do. As the Spirit has come up into consciousness, it started to dream with the aim of creating the Creation and, in order to dream it up, it has used up all the little pieces of *nothing* in the Universe.

Imagine a sunny day when you can see all the particles in the air. First, it is like nothing, but on a microscopic level, those are like fibres, and if you put a whole bunch of them together you will start to have *physical* matter. What brings it together in the first place is that it has been dreamed of in the mind of the Creator, like the *blueprint* of life, like when an architect makes a blueprint to build a house.

Any creation comes from the spirit that is holding things together. For example, if you take two stones and try to put them together, they are not going to hold together except if, in your mind, you find a way to put these two stones together. So, the work of *bringing together* all the bits of nothing until a physical mass emerges represents a huge effort; just like any project that starts from nothing.

The spirit of Sky Woman could be compared to the spirit of a mother. Any child comes with a spirit connected to the mother and to the rest of the Universe thanks to blood, which is the very first thing that appears when the fetus develops and the heart starts pumping. This is how Sky Woman gives us life: through the spirit and through love, which are one and the same.

When we are dreaming, or having an emotion, the different liquids that are released into our brain hold the physical and the spiritual worlds together.

The Universe is made of water. This water is also the blood of our Mother Earth in the same way it constitutes our own blood too. Without water, there would be no terrestrial bodies, no planets: nothing. All those things at a microscopic level have to be held together. And the *liquid* that holds all these things together is the spirit of Sky Woman. Absolutely everything in Creation is made of that Spirit. We could compare it to a hair: It only grows because it is connected to the body. If we pull it out, it will lose life, because it gets its spirit from the main body. Also, all the water (blood) of the Universe is governed by the moons, which in turn are generated by the love of women. The moons (fertile periods) give us life, so we honor what women gave to us.

The first thing that was created can't be said to have been designed as something specific, but as it formed, and as it began to grow, it started to duplicate itself. Duplication is reproduction. To reproduce is to give birth and only females can give birth, so the first thing that duplicated itself was female, otherwise it would not have been able to reproduce itself.

When Sky Woman fell from the Sky World, birds flew beneath her to slow her descent onto the Turtle's back. On a microscopic level, it could be compared to an ovule falling down from a fallopian tube and landing in the uterus that becomes a womb once it is impregnated. This womb is the Universe and the water represents the physical and the spiritual powers. In that blood, we find love and emotions too. The liquid forms the mass and maintains a connection between all that exists within Creation and between any molecules within the Universe. We are therefore the Universe, even if we cannot see it at the scale in which we find ourselves.

Once Sky Woman arrived on the Turtle's back, she needed some mud to be able to hold onto it, to stand on it. Many birds and different creatures tried to get some for her from the bottom of the ocean, but they died. Even the beavers tried. This is the reason why they are so important in the Chiefs' gatherings within the *Kaianerahsere'kó:wane skennen*, the Great Law of Peace and Understanding. Indeed, when the Chiefs get together, they must eat beaver's tail, an act that represents life in ways that people cannot imagine.

A flowing river is in constant motion; nothing accumulates. When the beavers come, they dam up that river, and the water becomes stagnant, then fish and other creatures can live in there, and then other animals come to eat those creatures, so it becomes a gathering place of Creation. This is the way the beavers provide life within Creation. Moreover, their tail represents the Law, given that the beaver uses it to slap the water and signal danger. But the beaver, although he tried to get mud for Sky Woman, did not succeed and died like the other creatures.

Because all these creatures gave their lives for Sky Woman within the process of Creation, in return she gave them important roles. They are like guests of honour when they take place at our table and are eaten, giving us their power and their energy.

Finally, the creature that succeeded in bringing back mud for Sky Woman is the otter. Once the mud had been placed on the Turtle's back, Sky Woman started to dance. Sky Woman, who put her love into everything, started to dance, shuffling her feet and creating the rest of the Creation.

When Sky Woman started to dance on the Turtle's back, she created the *individual identity*, which is another mind that she could interact and weave things with. Already, in this story, we can identify love. And the creatures that came to help Sky Woman represent emotions. All things are formed from there.

When Sky Woman planted her feet in the mud and started massaging the Turtle while dancing, she created on the back of the Turtle 13 squares representing the ceremonies and all the things that occur within the 13 cycles of the moon. Because Sky Woman landed on the Turtle's back, we could not say that we are talking of the beginning of the Creation. Where would the Turtle come from? There had to have been something before Sky Woman came in order for a Turtle to have been there.

Before Sky Woman came onto the Turtle's back, she had first created our Grandmother Moon—the beating heart of our Mother Earth. Moreover, every solar system has many moons within it. When we talk about our Grandmother Moon within the Creation story, we do not necessarily talk about the physical thing that we see when we look at the sky, but we talk about her role, not only here in relation to our Mother Earth, but the role that all moons play in relation to all the planets. The moons do the same thing in every part of Creation: planets get the blood (water) from them. We find the equivalent of the Moon within each molecule of skin where it initiates the process of pumping the blood into the skin. This is the way that the Moon is a continuous process that happens in absolutely every part of Creation.

So, Grandmother Moon gave life to our Mother Earth that had brought to life Taroniawakon and Sawiskera, the Twins. So first, there were three generations of females before males came into the picture: Sky Woman, Grandmother Moon and Mother Earth.

At the same time Creation is created, destruction is also established, because when life takes place, the knowledge of how to stop it is automatically created, which generates a very delicate balance between continuing life and stopping it. When Sky Woman creates the world, she knows that some strands are not right, but she could not take them out because they are her own children. And because the female has only the desire to love and to be loved, Sky Woman has to create the male (the Twins). It is they who interpret the love and emotions of the Creator by putting them into motion in this world. These are also the ones who support the Law and establish the order under the authority of women.

Taroniawakon and Sawiskera, the Twins, represent the blood lines of the Wolf Clan and the Bear Clan: Taroniawakon, the Wolf, and Sawiskera, the Bear. Of course the Turtle Clan is related to the Turtle onto which Sky Woman came. So, the Twins walk together five steps on the back of the Turtle; they separate and walk four steps, then they come back and walk together again. Each time they do this, it does the same as when a cell splits into two cells, then into four, and then into eight, and so on. Today, when we carry out the ceremonies, we duplicate the very first duplicating act within the physical creation.

In Creation itself, the continuous line goes like this: from Sky Woman to our Grandmother Moon, to our Mother Earth and to all the women from the newest-born baby girl to the eldest grandmother. All the women could mean 3 billion women on Earth. Even though all the women are identified as one body and one unit, there is a head: the Clan Mother who is a Chief. The authority of the women is polarized within this title, because it represents all women, regardless of the stage of evolution of each individual woman. The first female Chief is Sky Woman, who is also the first authority in Creation. So, the women hold the continuous authority within Creation, and this has gone from one generation to the next since the very beginning. Woman is constantly adjusting to the process of Creation, this is why she is always determining, and discovering, and establishing what the Law is because she knows what step to take next.

Anything that is created throughout the evolution of Creation was already determined billions of years ago from the blueprint. Of course, anybody can break the result that comes out of a blueprint: you can break the windows, burn the house, and then the result won't look like what was predetermined. If I built a house and I pass on this house to my children, then they have to stay faithful to the rules concerning how and why it was built.

Nobody has to believe our Creation story, and it does not have to make sense, though it does. In any case, anybody could say anything they want about it. Try to recount what happened the day that you were born. Can you? Maybe because somebody told you what happened on that day, but what would you say if you were the first human being? Nobody can remember their birth. Moreover, do you know somebody who remembers the first time they defecated? Of course, it could sound funny to think about this, but this first event is really significant, because after that event, we are completely out of the realm of where we came from where the food that we push out comes from inside of our mother. So, in pushing out the food that comes from the ancient realm in the new realm, there is no further spiritual connection to it. It may seem to be a physical thing, but it is a spiritual one too. Finally, nobody can remember what it was like when we were born, but the mothers can tell us, and for most of us they do, as does Sky Woman who communicates with her daughter through DNA.

Obviously, many parts of the Creation story are missing here. I can't recount in a book chapter what could take a complete day to say in a Recital. Of course, because of the 500 years of genocide thrust upon us, there are probably some parts that have been lost, in the same way the Spanish genocide upon the Mayan people wiped out the physical remnants of the *Popol Vuh* (Mayan Book of Council). This helps to explain why the information my people got may not be full and complete.

Finally, the only way we can tell what the beginning of the Creation was really like is by looking at the end result: the way that people are today. Compare those that live under matrilineal authority, under Sky Woman, to the people that put male domination first: the latter wage war against Creation.

The way that we understand Creation dictates the way that we will behave. I would say that the native people understand the way we came into this world a lot better than the others, because matrilineality provides tools in order to be in balance and har-mony with all life, respecting all Creation. Nevertheless, the way 7 billion people on Earth are conducting themselves under male-dominating science is destroying the Creation that we come from, which means that scientists understand nothing about anything.

Katsitenserio
Stuart Myiow Junior

Onowarake Kawehnoke
Turtle Island

First, Sky Woman gave birth to our Grandmother Moon. Then, she gave birth to our Mother Earth who gave birth to the Twins who are both male. These males are basically the hands of the Creator, and they do the work, as any creation needs hands to make that happen. When our Mother Earth gave birth to the second twin, she died in the process. Afterwards, the Twins buried her in the soil, and then tobacco grew from her mind, strawberries from her heart, corn from her breast, beans from her fingers, squash from her navel, potatoes from her toes, and so forth. Now, everything grows from our Mother's body.

Because tobacco has grown from our Mother Earth's mind, it is the form of communication, the method that we use to communicate with things (trees, animals and so forth) within Creation. Tobacco is equivalent to our thoughts or ideas in our own minds; it links us together on a spiritual level. This is why when the white men came, we offered them tobacco, but they have not used it correctly. They disrespected it like they disrespect the Earth.

All things on Turtle Island started at the South Pole, from the Earth's magnetic field, which is Earth's DNA. The dreams from the inner world came here, the outer world, creating the physical world. If people were aware of these things, and would work with them, they would be able to live in harmony with Creation, which is not separate from us.

Moreover, if we can dig up the Earth's belly, divert rivers, destroy the land, the water, the air and everything else, it means that we have the Creator's power. Since people have such a power, they have to know who, where, and when they are, and where they come from, in order to use such a power correctly without destroying Creation.

When Sky Woman fell onto the Turtle's back, she came to a precise physical place onto the Earth: the Southern Pole. This is where she began the steps in creating Creation. She kept her feet planted firmly on the ground and she danced to the Song of Creation, which is the heart of *Ionkiatishon* (the Creator) and this heartbeat can be heard everywhere throughout the Universe.

Everything, whether it is a planet or anything else in the Universe, has a heartbeat; there is a rhythm to the cycle of everything. When a planet is rotating, interacting with the rest of the solar system, it is a living thing, even when science might call it a cold dead planet. So, Sky Woman started to dance to this heartbeat, and as she shuffles her feet on the Turtle's back, she creates the Turtle. It is not like there was a turtle there, and then Sky Woman came and said: "Hey! Look at this turtle!" She created the Turtle at the same time she started to dance on it—the necessity of creation created it. This is a sort of self-creation. Probably if the poles would completely melt, we would see the 13 squares on the Turtle's back (Southern Pole), which would not be a good thing, of course.

From the moment Sky Woman began to dance on the Southern Pole, this part on the Earth began to rotate because she started to spin it, like a gear: click, click, click . . . Sky Woman thus started to turn the physical matter on its axis and started the *motor* of Creation. The push behind this rotation is the spirit of our Mother—it is also the push behind all life. She did it through her spirit, which is moving the physical Creation in the same way that a human being receives their spirit in the womb. Here, we are talking about how DNA was created and its rotary movement. So, as DNA started to rotate, it began to weave the structure of matter, which is woven between its two opposites.

The most important place on Earth—where all the continents are linked—is the Southern Pole, and the only continent that directly touches it, through an undersea mountain range, is Turtle Island (so-called South America). When we look at it on Google Earth we can see a baby turned upside down, prepared to be born into this realm; prepared to come out of the *underworld*, so to speak. This is where DNA begins. Anybody can see it on Google Earth, but if somebody does not know what they are looking for, then, they are not going to see it.

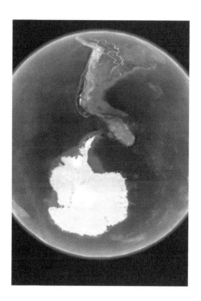

What we call South America is where Corn (Life) comes from. It has existed for over 10,000 years. Corn would not have moved here if those mountains had not been formed. The forming of those mountains was the beginning of the journey of Corn—the beginning of our identity, the beginning of us coming into being. The formation of this mountain range that starts from the southern pole is the original strand of the double helix of DNA.

Because the female came first, we can say that the southern part of the hemisphere is female, and the northern part is male, even if they both include the male and the female. And when we look at it on Google Earth, we can see that the mountain range of the east coast of the Americas is not as rugged as the western mountain range. These are the strands of DNA.

If you follow the western mountain range through to Venezuela, there is a place, over the Catatumbo River, where there is a constant electrical lightning storm known as Catatumbo Lightning. Ever since non-Native peoples came over 500 years ago, they have identified this phenomenon. At this specific place on Earth, there are more than 40,000 bolts across the night sky, for as many as 300 nights a year. This is where the DNA breaks off as a result of the electrical charge, which is emitted from the female hemisphere.

In the past, scientists used to think that the stronger spermatozoid swims to the egg and gets to fertilize it, but this is not true. In the 1980s (with the advent of the electron magnascope, which enables the observation of electrons) they found that a bunch of spermatozoids get to the egg, which then emits an electrical charge that selects the sperm that will be allowed to fertilize. So, the Catatumbo River is where the split in the DNA structure occurs; this is where the two strands of the Earth's DNA are created by the original female strand that divides and designates the second strand to be male.

People cannot see, but starting from this place, the mountain range goes down under the sea, turning in on itself to go on the west coast of North America, just like DNA turns: One strand goes under and one goes on top. The Maya identified this phenomenon, saying that everything was crossing over. Thus where the DNA splits is where the second phase of Creation began: when the male was created.

So we have female in the south and male in the north, and the west side of North America is male. That is the reason why the strand of DNA in the west is rough; an impenetrable environment (the Rocky Mountains). This strand of the DNA continues up to Alaska where the male goes haywire and where he is banished into the nighttime realm (the other side of the Earth) because he was as a serpent in the garden.

Alaska is where the DNA has been broken even if it was supposed to continue over the North Pole. As a result, the rest of the people in the world are connected to Turtle Island through a little underwater mountain range (the Aleutian Islands in southwest Alaska), which connects them to North America, South America, and then to the Antarctic.

The physical matter on Earth begins in one place: the South Pole. And it also ends there because it is not connected properly. As a matter of fact, every continent is connected from point A (the South Pole) to point B (the end of the Mid-Atlantic Ridge). Because we see the breakage of DNA, we could conclude that it is already predestined that sooner or later it will fail, but all evil, regardless of its size, can be fixed.

People could be sceptical of what is said in this chapter; anybody could look on Google Earth and not see the baby turned over and ready to be born. Besides, through the gestation process, the fetus in the womb of its mother knows exactly when it is time to turn upside down at approximately seven or eight moons, in order to be ready to be born into this world. If the fetus does not turn upside down, the baby could die and possibly also kill the mother. This natural process that directs us to turn upside down is encoded in the DNA of all of us. The whole journey of Creation is encoded into the Earth and into the Creation itself.

We are just learning to speak to the people who came from across the great waters in the last 500 years. It means that we have just learned how to communicate with them; I am not talking about the language, but the way they understand and see things. So, when we use Google Earth, we use their science to show and to prove to them what has been stated since the beginning of time.

When we have our ceremonies, we are participating with the very event of Sky Woman creating physical matter. Through our ceremonies we keep the body of Creation alive. This is the equivalent to the body mechanism which regenerates our skin or renews our blood.

If a person does not interrelate with that most sacred event, then this event is disturbed. This is what we are doing with women today: changing them from being the life givers into now being the life takers, as they can now join the army, pick up a gun and kill some other mother's child.

Science today talks about the Big Bang Theory, but no matter what they could say, clearly, there must have been something so sacred that had it not happened, none of us would be here.

In fact, there is not a particular name like Big Bang or anything else when we talk about the Creation. It is a process that flows and goes to wherever there is life: a continuous evolution. Anyway, as the Creation Story is usually only transmitted through oral tradition in a Law Recital, we can only have bits and pieces of it in this book. During a Law Recital, this teaching is more solid and complete.

One thing is sure, we have to know the Great Law of Peace, because it explains to us the directions in the Universe in which our six senses are the six points of reference. We have five points that are not adjusting, that are solid, and the sixth point is the one that can fluctuate; it is the one that we can identify as being intuition—the magic of women. Thanks to these six senses, we can triangulate exactly where we are. Within the magnetic field, direction is the main important thing. Nobody can go against that. Going in the proper direction allows us to establish left and right.

What if we don't teach our children about Creation; what if we don't show them how to interact with that? They are here to continue our work, but if we don't show them how to come back onto the right path, they will repeat our mistakes.

Every man must continuously speak about Sky Woman and must continuously teach the things he knows about her. It is the male's responsibility to understand the Creator and to interact with her, the same way that a man grows up and finds out that he has a responsibility toward his mother. Anyway, all things in Creation have responsibility toward their mothers.

If we enjoy life, and if we want to continue to play, to dance, to laugh, to run, to swim, to eat our favourite foods, and to do anything else that makes us happy, we must understand that all of these things come from Sky Woman. It is she who gives us the spirit, the body, and the power to do all those things. It is very important that the minds of the young people are taught the Creation story because it is their own story, and if we don't know our history, we don't know anything.

Katsitenserio
Stuart Myiow Junior

Tekanon'tsitote Oniare Tsini:iawenhsere
The Two-Headed Serpent Prophecy

While traveling the highways of life, quite often we come upon roadside hazard signs warning us of dangers. If we understand the symbols, we can adjust our driving speed, prepare our reflexes, and focus our attention on the approaching hazards. With a little luck and the power we have, we may very well maneuver around any roadside hazard that may come upon us.

However, if we are unable to understand the symbolic renditions on a roadside hazard warning sign, we might very well pass it by, not giving it our attention. Consequently, while we are busy speeding down the road, drinking our coffee, and leaning over to put a CD in the radio, our reflexes unprepared, we might very conceivably run right off of our path and even die, crashing head-on into the rocks.

In our last seconds of life, we may frantically search for another quarter to put into the machine, hoping another vehicle may pop out and enable us to continue our journey. But, unlike a video game, this game of life only has one vehicle that, when it crashes, the game is over. During that time, one's last thoughts may be: "What the hell did that sign say?"

With this scenario in mind, even a simple roadside warning sign is a prophecy, for the sign warns us to prepare for danger so that we may avoid it. This makes it clear to us that though a prophecy may actually be scheduled to happen, it does not mean that the worst possible scenario must happen. All prophecies come in two stages: the first stage being that of a warning of the danger of a catastrophe; the second stage being the actual catastrophe, if the warning is not heeded. Thus, the purpose of prophecy is to warn of danger, so it may be avoided.

However, in today's scientific world where real human concerns and spiritual beliefs take a backseat to so-called progress, a disbelief in prophecy has been placed in our minds through modern education and religion. This is based upon fear of the truth, which is very evident in the modern education of history since the first European contacted us. Even non-Native people are starting to realize that their version of just this small part of history is based on lies and one-sidedness. The truth is deeply feared, for if the truth about modern education (which is based upon science) was discovered and accepted it would hinder scientific progress, for the very purpose of scientific progress would then be put in question.

Therefore, in order to keep the masses under the control, science, through modern education and religion, had to embed deeply into our psyches the idea that the beliefs in prophecy are illogical and manifest themselves in some ancient shaman's mind through superstition, or through dreams and visions, or something of that sort. This has enabled science to explain that such a person would be highly susceptible to hallucinations or something equivalent; thereby discrediting the words of warning of a prophecy, regardless of how sensible these words may be.

Being that prophecies come from spiritual beliefs, when one denounces any prophecies received by a people, one also denounces their spiritual beliefs. Nevertheless, when we consider the fact that most races have spiritual beliefs that can explain how life started, its purpose and what roles we play within it—but science cannot— it should cause any rational person to wonder why we let such insanity drive the vehicle we are all riding in.

So here we are, letting something that not only cannot read the warning signs, but refuses to listen to the humans who can.

Tsiniiaʼwenhsere
The Prophecy

One day, a young boy found a two-headed serpent whose skin had beautiful colours with gold and silver stripes down its back, but it was very sickly, unable to care for and feed itself. It was on the verge of death. This was due to the fact that one head wanted to go left, while the other wanted to go right. One wanted to move, while the other wanted to stay still. Basically, one head didn't know what the other one was doing, and vice versa.

The young boy brought the serpent to his village. The elders were very cautious with it but everyone loved its beautiful colours and felt sorry for it. The young ones said: "It's so poor! How will it survive? Look at how helpless it is! Surely it will die with the coming of winter. Please let us keep it." The elders agreed saying: "OK, you can keep it, but not in the house, and remember: If you want to keep it, you will have to feed it."

The children fed it with insects but the snake wanted more so they fed it with field mice, but the snake wanted more. They fed it with rabbits and small birds, but the snake wanted more! Finally, with this serpent getting so big, the elders began hunting our brothers the beavers and otters to feed the snake. But, this snake didn't seem to get enough!

The serpent, now way too big to handle, began eating our dogs, then our food supply—the gardens and the deer, then all of our spirit guides. When that was not enough, the serpent finally began eating our people. It ate the children, the elders, and any who were not fast enough to get away. So horrible was this serpent that it even ate our dead—something that our people had never seen.

Then this two-headed serpent began eating whole villages and in the process, it enslaved many of our people. Then it started traveling the countryside looking for more villages to eat. Along the way, it started eating anything in its path—the forest, all the animals, and the countryside itself. It ate holes through mountains that were in its way and it poisoned our waters with its defecation.

After traveling the entire country, it began to backtrack to totally destroy the land by poisoning anything that may have been undisturbed. All the animals were completely poisoned, as was the ground. The forests that were missed were now completely devoured; the waters that were not damaged were now completely poisoned also.

Finally, after our Mother Earth was destroyed and there was nothing left for the two-headed serpent to consume, it then started to eat into the Sky World. It was said that it would make its way out to our Grandmother Moon, the night-time Sun, and that it would even try to destroy our Elder Brother, the Sun, and that from there it would attack all our cousins, the Stars. But it was also said that when the serpent would be near the end of its destruction of our Mother Earth, the planet would fight back to clean herself.

At this time, the serpent will be weakened by the natural powers released from our Mother's revolt. Revealing itself for what it really is, the serpent will create its own demise and begin to destroy itself. Through its own greed and its insatiable appetite for destruction, one head would begin to eat the other and the serpent would destroy itself through internal conflict and that all it had *enslaved to work for it to keep it alive would revolt against it.*

While the serpent would be distracted, a young boy would come again and with the power of the hair of the Clan Mothers he would make a bow that would thrust his arrows straight and true into the heads of the two-headed serpent. When the serpent would roll over and die, it is said that the young boy would climb atop the huge monster's belly, and in disembowelling it, all the real people who were eaten up would be released.

Once the serpent was destroyed, all life would once again live in freedom the way the Great Spirit had intended and Creation itself would blossom with a new vibrancy that has not been seen since the coming of the serpent.

This is basically what the Two-Headed Serpent Prophecy relates. Though it may sound like a fairy tale shrouded in myth, the fact remains it is the warning sign on the highway we are traveling together. We must remember that this prophecy was told to us by our ancestors before the coming of the white man. Yet the prophecy has predicted precisely everything that would happen, so any rational person should contemplate what the next stage of the prophecy is.

The prophecy states that the serpent will enslave our people. This proved to be true with our people being sucked into religion; the same religion that brutally murdered our ancestors. This also proved true with many of our people working for the government through band councils which are a disgrace to our ancestors and cause us to fight internally. The prophecy also stated that the serpent would kill our children, destroy our land, our water, the sky and then attack our cousins, the Stars. The true spirit of our children has been killed through residential schools and a brainwashing inflicted by an education of lies. The sky is already polluted to the point that it has depleted the ozone covering a huge part of our hemisphere. The ozone has been destroyed so much that vast amounts of harmful radiation are now permitted to penetrate everything on Earth, leaving everything in a critical life-threatening situation. The serpent has already violated our Grandmother Moon, mining her for helium-3. The assault continues with some projects to leave the Earth to inhabit and industrialize the planet Mars.

The prophecy states that near its end, the serpent will begin to initiate its self-destruction. We are seeing this happen as governments throughout the world fight among themselves, which weakens them. Church and state came into power by suppressing women from their organizations. Before, in Europe, women were *shaman*, spiritual leaders, healers and were highly respected and sought after for their great knowledge of the *real* things in life.

At that time, people were living within a matrilineal society (similar to ours) with clans that were passed down through the women, which gave everyone their identity and taught respect of the female entity. However, when the European man started going haywire, having visions of grandeur of ruling the world, he had to create a new religion and structure of leadership that would permit him to go against the teachings and peaceful leadership of the women.

In order to create a new identity that would permit him to go around acting like a bad boy, killing, stealing and raping, he had to enslave and destroy his old identity, so that no one would ever again be able to find out where the serpent came from. The state went on a murder campaign to remove those women who threatened them because they were directing their men to resist the suppressive governments. The church sanctified this murder campaign by calling these women witches, and labeled these murders *witch hunts*.

The church also had to murder these women because they threatened the church's male autocratic existence. The church knew that women are the true power that has the true divine connection with the Creator—not men who do not participate in the continuity of Creation in the way the Great Spirit intended.

Although almost everything that was predicted in the Two-Headed Serpent Prophecy has come true, it does not mean that the whole prophecy has to transpire the way it states. We must remember that if a prophecy is like a sign on the side of the road warning us of upcoming danger, there is no rational excuse to run head-on into the danger when it can be avoided. The end of the prophecy may represent a violent eruption of chaos that may appear to be inevitable, but if our people can remember their identity and return to the Great Law of Peace—the *true* way of life—we could begin to reverse the process.

Hearing some of the key points of the prophecy, one can easily see the connections to what is really happening in the world around us. But what good is it to know the prophecy if one does not know what to do or where to begin to reverse the process? We do not believe that this prophecy predicts the end of the world, as some prophecies from other cultures do, but we do believe that drastic changes to life will occur. Therefore, if we want to continue our existence within our present concept of life, there are certain things we should do.

All people should begin to question and make serious decisions about what they believe, what they think is good for the entire family of life, what they will support spiritually and politically. Also, they should question themselves about what lifestyle will accord them the way to practise their beliefs.

Native nations must stop seeking recognition from the federal government. Negotiations such as those initiated by a pseudo self-government[46] will only put our people under the control of the foreign government, leaving them without collective rights (tax-exemptions, border crossing, hunting and fishing, and so on.) If possible, they should also seek out the traditional councils on their reserves, or on the nearest reserve to them, and support them in their struggle against the elected councils; for it is these elected councils that are signing away all of our rights. This is why all Natives must support their traditional ancestral councils, for this is where the true fight is.

---

46. See note 14, page 70.

To conclude, the most crucial thing we can do to protect ourselves as Native people is to return to the ways of the Longhouse, support our traditional council and participate fully in the ceremonies, songs and dances. For it is these natural ways of life that will give us a deeper understanding of Creation and our roles within it.

Katsitenserio
Stuart Myiow Junior

Tsiioterahkwa'tehiaron'hatie
Grandmother Moon Teaching

All men of the Earth should know their roots and their origins. However, religion teaches us that God, a masculine image, created man first: Adam. What happened afterwards? The man was alone. So, God created woman. What does this mean for women? They are considered inferior. They are not the original design, according to the religion of men. And the worst that is taught is that mothers are inferior to their own sons. Of course, we all know that is not true. How can we still allow such structures when we know they are false? To find our roots, we must regain our hearts.

We live a in world constituted by three main things: the Earth, the Sun and the Moon. And there are two predominant things we see when we are looking at the sky from this world: all day long, it is our: Eldest Brother the Sun, and all night long, it is our Grandmother Moon. Every morning, when I get up, I touch the Sun, I kiss him and I kiss the Moon every night, but everybody cannot do that, because it has been removed from their identity. Our Mother Earth, our Grandmother Moon and our Elder Brother the Sun are our family. But when seen through man-made science, we notice that the female identity has been taken from our family.

Because it takes the female out of the equation through the process of theoretical understanding, man-made science refers to the Moon as a cold dead rock. When you only have a male dominant version of science in all aspects of life, everything you do is going to be wrong. That said, you will get immediate gratification; but then if you take any woman and put her in the same scenario, instead of looking for immediate gratification, she will probably look for long term happiness. And if you take the long term happiness of the female and the short term gratification of the male, and put them together, they will clash.

We cannot function from a male-dominant perspective of science or knowledge because it is short term. We should be functioning only with the balance between female and male: between long term happiness and short term gratification.

Because the male has locked up the female for thousands of years, we are living in a world of short term gratification. So we can dig up the ground, obtain some money, and have a party tonight! And tomorrow night, there is going to be a big hole here because we dug up the ground, and the women will be sitting around this hole and their long term happiness becomes long term unhappiness. The women have experienced long term unhappiness for thousands of years, since the beginning of male dominance.

In order to maintain the balance, women have to teach the young boys about patience and consideration for others from the time they are brought into this world. If boys don't have that, they go into the male-dominant school, and no matter how much they love their mothers, they will learn to oppress her. This is short-term gratification. But the Moon teaching is long term. It teaches us how to identify Sky Woman, our Grandmother Moon, our Mother Earth, and all the women from the newest born baby girl to the eldest grandmother, because they are all the mothers of our nations. There is no difference between the newest born baby girl, the eldest grandmother, our Mother Earth, our Grandmother Moon and Sky Woman herself.

According to the Great Law of Peace, it is illegal for a man to separate a woman from her mother. But under male dominance, when a woman gets married, she usually leaves her mother. The males are conditioned this way, so when a man marries somebody, he takes her away from her home which forces the woman to raise her child away from her mother, away from her aunts, away from their grandmother. It is not supposed to be that way. There is no woman who is supposed to be raising her children on her own; she is supposed to be raising her children with her mother, her grandmother, and her aunts are supposed to be around. When a man marries a woman, he is supposed to live in the nation, the community, the family of this woman.

In many families in the world, when the child is 18, he is thrown out of the house. My own uncle was saying: "Ah! My daughters, when they are going to be 18, they are no longer my problem. They have to go out of my house." This uncle was in the Korean War II. Supposedly to be fighting for freedom, love and family, and then coming home to tell your daughters that, as soon as they are 18, they have to get out of the house: this is nonsense.

Across the ocean, there are many countries where the men marry their daughters off to some rich men and send them away; they sell their own daughters. Can you see the insanity in that? People don't see or understand how they have become cut off from their humanity through male dominance, which is an abomination.

Today, people are living alone in single homes. If a father is under pressure to support his family then, yes, he could get to a point where he says to his daughter that she has to get out of the house. At the same time, this man is the king in his castle and can do whatever he wants. It is in these single houses that males have given themselves the power to be violent toward the females. In the Longhouse, all people live together. There is less pressure on everyone, and the women have their full power in there; they cannot be abused. Nobody beats up a wife when he is in a group. In that context, no woman can get raped either.

Ionkhisotha aonthen:kha karah:kwa
Grandmother Moon

We all come from a fetus. We all know that babies, when they arrive in this world, have a small body with a big round head. When we see them, we do not think about the way in which they have developed. What developed first? Is it the left leg, the right arm, a lung, a rib, the rib of Adam for a woman to come from? The first thing that developed, of course, is the heart because no matter what part of the body develops next, it will need blood to grow. Therefore, the fetus begins to develop in the heart. So when we understand this, we understand that this is also the way that Mother Earth has developed: the Moon came first because she is the heart of the Earth.

Moreover, we all know that the Moon revolves around the Earth. So, when it is full, the Moon is positioned in line with the Earth and the Sun, and the Earth is in the middle.

FULL MOON

When the Moon is placed this way, one of its hemispheres is located far from the Sun. This far side of the Moon remains, at all times, away from us since the Moon never revolves around herself; she remains permanently in her position, always smiling to the Earth. Nevertheless, a lie circulates about the *dark* side of the Moon, because when the Moon is on the other side of the Earth, the side that we believe is dark is facing the Sun. It is then the side facing us that becomes dark. One should therefore speak of the far side of the Moon instead of the dark side of the Moon.

If Earth were closest to the Sun, even only a few kilometres closer, we would see the entire ecosystem at risk, since these few kilometres would be enough to cause a radical temperature change. Moreover, the distance between the position of the Moon when full and its position when it is new is approximately 800,000 kilometres. That distance generates a huge difference in temperature on the Moon.

When the Moon is full, she is at her furthest position from the Sun. What happens to its most distant hemisphere? It cools. What do we do when we are cold? We contract. So, when the far side of the Moon is far from the Sun, it contracts.

When the Moon comes close to be full, we see more and more of her, and we unconsciously associate that to expansion associated with an object that has heated up. Naturally, we think that the Moon is getting hotter, as we associate light with heat, but the reality is the opposite.

Then, at the New Moon phase, when the Moon goes in the opposite position, what happens to its far side from the Earth? It is facing the Sun and being heated by it. What happens to us when we are very hot? We sweat.

NEW MOON

Then, when the far side of the Moon is near the Sun, the Moon expands and sweats, even if at the exact moment of the New Moon, we don't see anything, and it appears that there is no Moon.

When we see the Moon going from the new Moon phase to the full one, we think that the Moon is expanding, because it becomes larger and lit up, but it is the opposite since the Moon moves away from the Sun, which cools her and makes her contract.

To summarize, when the Moon is full, her far side freezes and she contracts. When the Moon in her path approaches the Sun, she warms up and expands. Thus, when we see the Moon through the phases, she becomes big, then small, big, small—expansion, contraction, expansion, contraction, and so on. As the heart that is in our bodies, it expands and contracts. That's all it does: inflates and contracts.

When this is the time of the New Moon, she approaches the Sun, heats and sweats. At the same time, the Sun always sends to Earth, second by second, solar winds that brush against the Moon on their way through.

EXPANSION DURING NEW MOON PHASE

These solar winds are basically electrons and protons that travel everywhere throughout our solar system. If we throw water into a strong wind, it will go in the direction of the wind. When Grandmother Moon expands, she perspires. Her sweat, coming from condensation, emerges from her body, and is captured by the solar winds that brush against the Earth and reach, in 14 or 15 days (according to the cycle), the opposite position of the Moon when full.

When the Moon is full, nothing blocks the solar winds that directly hit the Earth. At that time, it is the Earth that is heated and is sweating in turn.

CONTRACTION DURING FULL MOON PHASE

We can then see the Earth's condensation: fog. Because this sweating is in our sights, we are able to observe the Earth transpiring. And even if we were a hundred metres, or even at the limits of our atmosphere, we could still witness this phenomenon. It would even be possible to see the condensation leaving the atmosphere. When it does, it is collected by the solar winds that project it directly onto Grandmother Moon, who captures it on her beautiful face.

The Equator is the part of the Earth that is the nearest to the Sun. This is where she sweats all the time. We can feel it, as it is always hot and humid in these areas. So, the *sweat* of the Earth (condensation) goes up into the atmosphere at the same time the solar winds come and penetrate it, going right through the Earth, and then right through the Moon. But also, the winds that don't go through the Earth catch the condensation that rises up.

To recap, the solar winds come, they hit our Mother Earth, picking up the sweat, they go through the atmosphere, and then are directed straight onto the face of our Grandmother Moon, who is at that moment in Full Moon phase.

So, this is how water, the outcome of our Mother Earth's sweat, is captured by Grandmother Moon. Then, when the Moon continues on her path around the Earth in direction of new Moon phase, she heats up, expands, and then the speed of her motion generates a centrifugal force that pushes the water—the blood of the Earth—through her body. What is happening when that blood appears from the body of the Moon and then returns to the Earth? It is clean and oxygenated. And again, the solar winds catch her sweat and bring it to the Earth. The far side of the Moon is where water comes out in its purest form.

Therefore, there is always a continuous link between our Grandmother Moon and our Mother Earth. This water that flows between the two is the umbilical cord, as a fetus in the womb of their mother is also connected. Almost nobody is aware of that link anymore.

In 2012, satellites were sent to map the dark side of the Moon. These satellites have detected what they called anomalies that they associate with geological activity that generates long strips on the Moon. Every woman who has carried a child, or anyone who is overweight, knows what stretch marks are. These bands are caused by the Moon's expansion when it approaches the Sun, the same as how the belly of a pregnant woman acquires stretch marks because of its expansion.

As we said, there are three predominant things in Creation: our Grandmother Moon, our Mother Earth and our Elder Brother the Sun. But from the Earth, however, we always only see the Sun and the Moon when we look at the sky. When we were younger, we could see a lot more stars than what we can see right now. For the last hundred years, all our relations that we could see at night have become almost invisible, because now the light is all down here: artificial light. It even takes away our ability to see out into the atmosphere. That creates a daytime atmosphere during the nighttime. The daylight provided by our Elder Brother the Sun is male. To have the daylight during the night brings us into a male-dominant imbalance.

For women, one of the most important things is the Moon Teaching. After the women have gone through that, they have a stronger sense of their femininity and of their relationship with our Mother Earth, our Grandmother Moon, Sky Woman and men. This teaching empowers women and leads them not to be subordinate, but to actually be the authority. In any case, the first teaching anybody should receive is the Moon Teaching because that gives them a solid identity; It lets them know where our heart is and what that thing we see in the sky at night is.

 Katsitenserio

Stuart Myiow Junior

Ie'iontate'rahkwa'kaias Ion'kha'sotha
The Moon Assailed

In 2009, NASA launched the first lunar mining competition called The Lunabotics Mining Competition (now simply called Robotic Mining Competition) that aims to generate "innovative ideas and solutions, which could be applied to actual lunar excavation for NASA."

Google is also sponsoring a Moon-related prize, The Lunar X-Prize, a $40 million competition to encourage privately funded teams to land a robot safely on the Moon, move 500 metres on, above, or below the Moon's surface and send back HD-TV Mooncasts for everyone to enjoy!

Newt Gingrich, presidential aspirant in the 2012 Republican contest, wanted to see a permanent Moon base established by the second term of his presidency, something that could be used for space tourism and mining ventures.[47]

Our Grandmother Moon is undergoing attacks. In fact, through United Nations agreements, China, the US and other countries have obtained the power to go to the remote hemisphere of the

---

47. http://www.mining.com/china-is-taking-lunar-mining-seriously-65595/

Moon to exploit helium-3. We already see the consequences of the male insanity imposed on the Earth by resource exploitation. What are the consequences of exploiting the resources of Grandmother Moon? The male cannot supply power for himself; he needs the female because he is too corrupt and lazy. He needs the power of women to exist in this world.

One kilogram of helium 3 would provide enough energy for a city the size of Houston for a year. You know what that means? It means tons and tons could be extracted in order to feed several cities and several economic systems.

Unlike Earth, which is protected by its magnetic field, the Moon has been bombarded with large quantities of helium-3 by the solar wind. Private enterprise is also interested in extracting water rather than helium-3. Indeed, the Shackleton Energy company envisages providing propellant for missions throughout the solar system using lunar water.[48] All the people that do not have the knowledge about the reality of the Creation, from within their original identity, are negative to Creation, and they are going to damage and destroy Creation.

Where helium-3 was found, on the far side of the Moon, the blood (water) is at its purest, its strongest form. Pushed out by the centrifugal force, it has been cleaned through the body of our Grandmother Moon. How long will the far side of the Moon last? How much time is left before the Moon is consumed? Especially now that there is privatization of the Moon and space publicly funded by everybody on Earth. The International Space Station is funded by the United Nations, which means almost everybody: the US, Britain, Russia, China and the European Union, and so on. They are all carrying out a direct assault on our Grandmother Moon, which means they are tearing apart the heart of our Mother Earth.

In 2012, we heard on the radio that people of NASA had a meeting in Québec city, at the Château Frontenac. We went there.

---

48. http://www.esa.int/Our_Activities/Preparing_for_the_Future/Space_for_Earth/
Energy/Helium-3_mining_on_the_lunar_surface

They were terrified when we arrived. There was a big ballroom with big doors. When we walked up to those doors, some people came running at us; they were so nervous, like if we were terrorists or something like that. We were five: a woman, my father, another old man, Yvan Bombardier and me. We brought a document to warn NASA to stay off of the Moon.

I personally spoke to a couple of scientists there; one was from France and the other from Belgium. When I told them to stay off the Moon because they don't know what they are messing with, they laughed in my face and told me that what I was proposing was science fiction. They also told me that they are not planning to go to the Moon. Then, I asked them to explain to me why they promoted a world-wide contest for somebody to develop a Moon excavator. They still laughed in my face.

If the world knew and understood what is going on, nobody would let happen what we, as a duped species, are currently imposing on the Moon.

Why has there been so much movement taking place at the International Space Station: 19 flights in 17 days during the month of August 2014? What went up there? What the hell are they doing there? They are preparing to launch an economic assault on our Grandmother Moon.

On Earth, we are not even aware of what is happening on the Moon. Because all this occurs on the far side of the Moon, no one will ever see, no one will ever know what is going on there. Out of sight, out of mind. We are just going to start to feel funny, to feel different. We are going to see strange things happening, like parts of the Earth dying.

To mine the Moon the way they do is not something that is in balance with the female aspect. This is a capitalist venture under male dominance. Male means economics, democracy, and insanity in this world. Ask women if they agree with the idea of mining the Moon, and they would say *No*.

What can we do? We can reach as many people as possible. To accomplish that task in the time frame in which we have seems impossible, but we must never look at what we cannot do; we must look at what must be done. And if we look around, we will arrive at the obvious conclusion that nobody else is on this same path; nobody else is identifying these things, nobody else is aware of what is happening. It would seem to others to be an illusion in our heads, like some grandiose vision.

Well, you don't have to believe me, I could be saying anything I want to you, and I could be lying through my teeth to you. But I challenge you to prove me wrong. If you leave all that information unchallenged, you will never know the truth. If it is a false belief in our heads, then what is the downside to even talking about that or spreading the knowledge? The downside would be that we say nothing. If we know what we know, and we believe it without saying anything, we would let the rape of our Grandmother happen, while doing nothing to stop it.

Of course, if we talk about the Moon, we can mine it as some kind of rock, but if we talk about our Grandmother, the beating heart of our Mother Earth, a part of our family, can we really mine her to obtain helium-3 for profit to sustain male dominance? We can't.

At this point, we should get angry. We should take that anger and direct it to do what we know, what we believe cannot be done. All the people on the Earth have never gotten together and said let's do this. They have been manipulated for a very long time. The result of this manipulation spreads like cancer.

The school system provides fragmented knowledge. For instance, I can look at my aunt sitting in front of me, and contemplate her beautiful face, but if I have a global vision, I could see a man pointing a gun in her face. The school system, academia—so-called education—focuses on the beautiful face without considering the gun pointed at it, without looking at the reality. So it is a lie: false information.

One of the first things that male dominance did to our identity was to take away the knowledge of the connection between the Moon, the Earth, and all the women, by murdering them for teaching the realities of Creation to their peoples. They have been killed for being what they called *witches*. For telling the truth, all these women have been killed. And no one has ever addressed these heinous crimes against all humanity by bringing these murderers to the so-called justice system. These crimes were instead allowed to happen in order to spread fear, hatred and war throughout all Creation, not just here on Earth! That is how they have silenced the voices of women that they have locked outside of their identity as the authority in Creation, in addition to deconstructing what they had created. The corrupt male mind has oppressed the female so completely that the female is now doing the same as the male, to other women, and she is also teaching it to her children. Therefore, children, young girls, grow up to fight against women.

Our children must be taught the Moon teachings, and moreover, they must be taught that when they were a fetus, at the very beginning of their lives, males were all first female. Then it would be easier for any human being to understand and to accept the reality of the female being: the original first being from whom the male came.

To understand the Moon teaching, you need to know the Two Row Wampum, which is not a political agreement between two peoples; it is an interface that creates balance between two opposites. And fundamentally, between women and men, the interface is love. But today, it is war and oppression.

Every time I speak like this, there are always women who do not agree with what I say. They tell me that they have not been oppressed: they are free, they go to school, they have careers; they can join the army, have a gun in their hands . . . for what reason? To kill other women's children? They are so equal, but consider that men can never be equal to women who came before men. Even in the Creation story, it is said the male came after three females. We first had Sky Woman, our Grandmother Moon, our Mother Earth, and then the male Twins came. So what does that mean if women have the right to do the same that men do? Does it mean equal rights? It means that you must climb down the evolutionary ladder. Of course, women cannot do that physically, but it is done psychologically. This means now that the women have oppressed themselves. And at the same time, we still have missing and murdered women all around the world.

When religion began, the first thing men had to do was to attack the female, to kill the spirit of women, because they are the power, the authority. Even within my people, there are many who believe in religion, no matter what it has done to them.

Today, the only solution we have is to shoot our arrow right into the heart of the enemy like in the Two-Headed Serpent Prophecy. When the serpent had consumed almost everything, a young boy comes along and, with the hair of a Clan Mother, he strings his bow, and then he uses it to shoot his arrow straight into the heart of the serpent. After, he slices open the belly of the serpent, and all the children that the serpent had eaten came out. This is where we are now.

If we are dissociated from the knowledge of our Grandmother Moon, the beating heart of our Mother Earth, then we have no problem blowing up bombs on the Moon; we have no problem extracting her so-called resources which are her vital life forces. The Moon Teaching gets the mind thinking straight; it helps to separate truth from lies. With this teaching, you are able to have proper politics that return the women back to their true identity and power. So they may once again maintain the balance and bring peace back to all Creation.

Katsitenserio

Stuart Myiow Junior

Ie'karahkwa'ieri A'sonthen'ne Wate'rihwah'tetiaton
Full Moon Ceremonies

At every one of its cycles, every 28 days or so, Grandmother Moon illuminates us with her great splendour. Traditionally, women would gather every New and Full Moon night after sunset to share any specific knowledge about femininity. Grandmothers transmit their wisdom to girls, young women and mothers. With *Kanienke'ha'ka* people, the connection between Sky Woman, Grandmother Moon and our Mother Earth extends to every woman. Women are therefore naturally in communion with the environment, medicines[49] and food.

In a Full Moon Ceremony, we gather around a fire after sunset on the night before, or on the exact night, or on the night after the Full Moon. Even if, for any reason, you cannot make a fire, you can gather and make a ceremony. Le Drapeau de la Famille[50] in collaboration with the Mohawk Traditional Council

---

49. See note 1, page 18.
50. Organization which aims at reconciliating and bringing together people of different origins (the great universal family).

of Kahnawake organizes a Full Moon Ceremony on every eve of the Full Moon on Mont-Royal in Montréal. This allows people of Montréal and elsewhere to learn about one of our traditional teachings.

It must first be noted that the ceremony does not belong to anyone in particular; it belongs to all the people. No one *holds* this ceremony more than the others. The purpose of this gathering is to collectively thank the female entity; it is to reconnect with our Grandmother Moon, with our Mother Earth, with Sky Woman and with all the women.

First, the people take their place in the circle. If members of this circle are part of a clan, they must have their backs in the direction relative to their clan. Being Wolves, for example, we place our backs to the north.

Before the ceremony, we smudge with sage. Usually it is women who are in charge of medicines. Therefore, a person, ideally a woman, circulates inside the circle with sage, and thus each one is smudged. Everything in the circle follows the order of Creation and flows in a counterclockwise direction.

In a recent gathering in Ottawa, we danced in a circle. We did it in clockwise direction, as we were in Anishnabe territory. It's the way they do it and I respect it. However, when I act from my identity, to honour it, I move in a counterclockwise direction, for it is in this direction that everything in Creation runs, even in the infinitely small.

Scientists have confirmed what we have always known when they speak of the existence of what they call molecules and atoms. The atomic structure rotates counterclockwise as do tornadoes, the Earth, the Moon, and the solar system. The double helix of DNA itself, scientists confirm, rotates counterclockwise. That is why we (the *Kanienke'ha'ka*) circulate counterclockwise in circles, dances and so on.

After smudging has started, tobacco is distributed. It is used to receive our intentions, our thoughts and our spirit. Each person takes a pinch of tobacco with their left hand and brings it to their heart. Once everyone has tobacco, someone again goes around the circle, ideally a woman, and the person collects the tobacco impregnated with our intentions, making of them a collective intention, so our minds become as one. Then the tobacco is offered to the fire, but before we do it someone says *Ohenton Kariwatehkwen*, the words of thanks that come before all else. This is how we open the ceremony.

Afterwards, a feather, usually an eagle feather, circulates. The person holding the feather expresses gratitude in the way that suits them, whether speaking in the language of their choice, singing, or remaining silent for as long as they need to. Once they have finished, they hand the feather to the person on their right. To be respectful, all others remain completely silent while someone is speaking. No one interferes, interrupts or disrupts in any way. Nobody finishes the sentence of someone else, even if they seem to look for a word. What the individuals want to speak has to come out of them, and nobody has the right to interfere in the way it comes out. The feather goes around only one time, so one has to take the opportunity to express themselves while it is there.

During the ceremony, there are a lot of things that we have to be thankful for, but we have to stay focused on the reason why we are at the ceremony: for our Grandmother Moon, for the female line, and to bring back the balance within Creation by bringing the women back to their natural seat of authority within the peoples.

When everyone has spoken, the speaker pronounces closing words, and people take the time to salute everyone before leaving. Usually the first who held the feather starts with the person to her or his right and runs into the circle counterclockwise to greet, hug, and thank everyone. Then, the person who was at the right, and who was greeted first, does the same, and so on until everyone has been greeted.

When the ceremony is held on Mont-Royal, sometimes passersby approach to see what is happening. Everyone in the group has the responsibility of keeping the circle healthy and safe; so we must quietly go to talk to the passersby, and to explain what is happening.

It also happens that people arrive at the ceremony once the circle is started. In this case, it is important to open the circle to these people to enable them to integrate into their rightful place; that is to say, where the feather has not yet been passed, in order to enable these people to also express themselves.

During the Moon Ceremony, we can give thanks for any little simple things that are important to us. For instance, for me, swimming in the moonlight, walking in the garden at night, and being able to see the corn growing under the beautiful face of our Grandmother Moon, or just sitting with the girl that I love, and seeing her beautiful face shine in the moonlight. I am grateful for all of these things.

In the daytime, we see things under daylight, but at night, in the brightness of our Grandmother, we see things in a different way. It shows us that there are different perspectives from which to see. And so we ask our Grandmother Moon to help us to see these things, to not stay focused on our own perspective, but to help us to attain the ability to look at things from a different perspective. This way, we can get the true picture, the true information of whatever we are looking at.

Also, we could ask our Grandmother Moon to help us to get our minds to function properly, to bring the balance into our minds, and to remove the imbalance of male dominance by bringing us back to all that has been chased away: love, kindness, beauty and logic. All these things have actually been expelled from humankind, out of the world. Of course, there is still much beauty in this world, but the negative that people are doing destroys this beauty.

We could also ask our Grandmother Moon to continue to work with the ancient Turtle, to continue to shake its back, to continue to remove all these unnatural creations that are destroying our Mother Earth, so her health can return.

Moreover, we could ask our Grandmother Moon to light and brighten the path of the people who are living in darkness, to lead them out of the darkness. We could also ask her to show the people once again the very core of their being, of their existence, where we come from, so we can find our rightful place in our family and stop its destruction.

We could give her thanks for the beautiful ceremonies, for the different things that have taken place within the last moon cycle, for everything that we have experienced, even the negative things that we remember, in order to draw lessons from them and keep those bad things from repeating themselves.

We could also ask our Grandmother Moon to bring back people to the council process so they could have access to the truth once again. We could ask her to return and to rekindle the Women and Men Council Fires, so that the directives of the women can be transmitted to the men who could take actions on the things that have to be addressed, those that are confronting our humanity and our identity.

We could ask her for guidance to interpret the ceremonies in a more profound way, as with the songs. We could ask her for the people to continue to receive the messages from the Messengers of the Creator, in addition to giving the people the ability to understand these messages that they receive, so they can act on them, in order that we may become human again, bringing back happiness and love into each of our individual daily experiences.

We draw our collective identity from our individuality, based on what the community chooses to do. The Grandmother Moon knowledge represents an obvious contrast to the male dominance model that isolates and grants individual and groups with particular interests (the riches, the one percent) with the power to direct the community and determine what will happen to all. Obviously, this behaviour always generates bad situations, since it concerns only a few families who give themselves personal rights over other individuals, and who place themselves above the Law by being able to buy the right to live their way through a corrupt judicial system.

The Full Moon Ceremonies should come back into the hearts and minds of everyone. They can be done with friends, family, whoever wants to share this moment. Thereby, from one cycle to the next, the people will walk upon our Mother Earth protected, with strength, with love, supporting each other, listening to each other, interconnecting our human experience, and rebuilding our collective identity.

Taiorah'kwen'hatie
Last Quarter

Universal Balance

To identify problems is a priority, but that would be pointless if the solutions were not also prioritized. Some dedicate their lives to the well-being of our Mother Earth. Here they have the opportunity to talk about it.

Tioronhiate
Grandfather Stuart Myiow

Kahwatsei're A'seiata'tiste
To Protect the Family

When I was young, there were white Francophones living across the river. They were left to themselves; the government did not help them. Their house was near mine and naturally we grew up together. They learned to speak English and we learned to speak French. They learned how to fish and to cook; they learned to collect berries and medicine.

One day, one of them came running up to tell me that a white man was fishing on the land. I told him "Well, you know what to do . . . " So he ran over there, and he threw the fishing rod and the white man into the water. He said this man had no business there. My friend became so much a part of the family that he lived as if he were Mohawk. So you can see that we are not savages like some have said. If we were, you would not be here today.

Growing up as a child was not easy. At school, I was prohibited from speaking to my relatives because they were traditional. The priests even told us not to look at them because what my relatives were doing was bad. I never listened and have always questioned every lie that those priests told us. It's no surprise that I was always in trouble with the teachers. They would tell us that they'd call our parents to ask them to whip us, but I would tell them, "Go ahead!" Nothing of the sort ever happened.

Today, this continues, but through the so-called justice system that is extremely corrupted. So when we speak the truth, we do wrong, but if we lie like their laws, we are righteous.

In the past, my sons used to go to the golf club to carry the golfers' equipment. One of them, about seven years old at the time, walked back home first, leaving behind his elder brother who had not finished work yet. On his way, an individual confronted him. He wanted my son to do bad things with him. He told him "If you don't do it, I am going to kill you." My son refused to do so.

When I got home after work, my wife told me that our son had not returned home, and no one knew where he was. So, I went to find him. I looked all over the bush, the golf course, and under the bridge. Without knowing it, I was right next to him. He was unconscious. On the golf course, in a sand trap, there were big pieces of wood with spikes. That animal took a piece of wood, beat my son until he scalped him, and left him for dead.

The next day, a golfer's ball fell near my child. I was still looking for him all over, when somebody came to tell me that my son was found, and that he and my wife were already on their way to the hospital. When I learned that, I drove at about 100 miles an hour to reach them—trust me, no police could have ever stopped me. At the hospital, they fixed my son. I told my boy I would not shave or cut my hair until we found that man.

Later, we were having a car ride when my son cried to me to stop. "Dad! I see him!" He showed me where, so I parked my car. The guy was painting while standing on a ladder: "Hey!" He turned around. I then checked with my son who confirmed that it was this man. I asked him to come down, so he did. I told him to explain what he had done to my son and to show me where. Then we went to the golf course. Once we got there, I hit him and knocked his teeth out. After that, all I did was drive him to the police. When the cops had him in their car, they asked me to beat him, but I refused.

We ended up in court. Our lawyer did not let me or my wife come to the courtroom. During the process, he came out and asked us if we were traditional. I told him, "What does that have to do with it?" but he turned around and went back into the courtroom without answering.

In the process, there was a priest who succeeded in getting the accused free because his father was a Knight of Columbus.[51] It was absurd. It was better that I not cross paths with this *animal* on the streets.

Once he was freed, he killed a person. They got him out again, and he killed another person. All this was because of the corruption of the Catholic Church and its priests—the same priests who kidnapped our children and inflicted the residential schools upon us[52].

This criminal, who ended up living in Toronto, had been released thanks to the help of a priest who molested young boys himself. And when that priest died, the Knights of Columbus buried him in the ground in front of the church. So, that is Christianity. You want me to join that? Never! What this story proves is that we should not trust that force. They don't know what they are preaching because if they did, they would not act the way they do.

Arizona

In the early '70s, I built my garage at home in Kahnawake to repair cars. I earned a good living that way for four or five years. I brought back a minimum of $1,000 per week, which was a lot back then because we were going through a recession. My father also had a garage where he sold gasoline.

Shortly after the construction of my garage, my sons, Kevin and Keith, and my nephew, Gordy, tried to convince me to take them to Phoenix because there was ironwork for them there. It took me a week to make my decision because it is a 3,900 mile trip (about 6,200 kilometres), but I had a good car.

When I got there, I drove everyone to work and I also worked. I did not really want to go because I had my garage and I was working

---

51. Order of lay Catholics.
52. See note 20, page 86.

with the traditional Chief in Kahnawake. It was not an easy decision to make. I felt that I was escaping our problems. However, I chose to stay in Arizona to work and I called my wife to ask her to join me with Gordy's wife and my youngest son, Stuart.

Several people from Kahnawake went to the southern states to work in Texas, New Mexico, California, and Arizona. Salaries were good; I earned about $1,500 a week working as a welder. The local people, who were supposed to be experts, were fired mostly because they did not take their work seriously. I was lucky, but certainly not lazy. There were even the Warriors who had come to work there, but the atmosphere was: "You'd better mind your own business and not disturb me, otherwise, watch out!"

Another thing that explains my decision to travel so far from home: Some Warriors had tried to kill us. In 1975, some people left the Longhouse fearing reprisals from the Warriors. The hostilities had led children to harass my son, Stuart, who was 12 at the time. He was constantly threatened. Parents had corrupted the minds of their children by teaching them hatred and anger.

If a dog is raised up in hatred and anger, it makes an aggressive attack dog that should be chained or it may bite someone. This represents the Warriors. They were trained from a young age to carry hatred and anger without logic for no reason other than the dictatorship of their Chief. He's the one who ordered them to eliminate anyone who would stand in their way. There were three men standing there: us—that is to say my sons and I—with a woman: my wife. In 1978, my son Keith, who was 20, was attacked by the Warriors. They were quite a group and seriously injured him. Moreover, they shot at our house, and my wife was nearly struck by a bullet.

No one else in Kahnawake—or even in the Confederacy territories—could resist the Warriors. They kept people in fear. My family was a threat to them, since we preserve the knowledge of the Longhouse. And those who know and keep the Law of the Longhouse are threatened by any corrupt group.

While we were in Arizona, we had some respite from the situation, and our family ties were strengthened. Nevertheless, my wife still had the title of female Chief and she received news from the community regularly. We received several boxes of information about Kahnawake that people sent without us even asking for them. The other Chief, the one with whom I worked, stayed in Kahnawake. He was left to himself, which was difficult for him.

We returned home six years later. Back home, I continued to work in my garage, but business was not very good. That's when I went to work in Brooklyn as an iron worker[53] until 1987. My father, my brothers, and my son, Stuart, like many of us, had done this work; we would return to Kahnawake on the weekends.

Because we had no fear of heights, Mohawks were famous in this field. Yet, there is nothing to be proud of because we built the machine now destroying our Mother Earth, in addition to separating us from our families. That's what the white man taught us: The travel that allowed us to work and earn money to support our families actually keeps us away from them.

The Warriors we knew in the '70s were the same when we returned to Kahnawake in the '80s. They had not changed. The constant threat of war hung over our heads. If we had stayed on the reserve, we would have been killed. Besides, this is what dictates the Great Law of Peace and Understanding: When war threatens us, the only answer is to get away from it unless you are absolutely forced to participate. We are people of peace; we do not want to hurt anyone. That's what the white man did not understand when he arrived here. None of us wanted to be in his presence, because he carried war with him. This is why indigenous peoples began to move away, but where could they go? The whites were everywhere. Then, at some point, the First Nations started to fight for their territories.

Having arrived in early 1990, we were wondering how we had survived until then. After overcoming this hardship, today we can no longer afford to make bad decisions, or to devote our energy to things that are not important. We only have one arrow in our quiver. We must launch it directly into the heart of the enemy.

---

53. To build skyscrapers.

Thónatéhontsok:te
The Man With No Land

My people like to have fun. For example, we like to play lacrosse. It is not just a game. White people adopted it as a sport, although it is traditionally a medicine[54] game. In my nation, we brought sick people to attend the match. To see that medicine game, to watch the players running and to check the ball going from one side to the other—all this excitement gave the sick the courage to walk again.

When the white man came, we were there to welcome the newcomers. We did not kill them. They were sick, they were dying and my people saved them. Thanks to our medicines, we gave them life again. Somewhere along the line, the white man forgot about that. This is where the trouble started between our peoples.

A few hundred years ago, terrible things were done by the white people. They stole corpses of my people from their graves. We wondered why white people were stealing our corpses. The goal was to bring them to study in Europe. For the whites, Natives were a great specimen; they were healthy and strong.

We never had official grave markers to say that a dead body was there. And we never believed in desecrating a body after it was dead. But imagine if you had a young child who died. You bury him or her, and somebody steals the corpse. If you weren't already hurt enough, you're now broken without the possibility of correcting the situation. This is the rape of life in our Mother Earth. When a woman is raped, every day, she dies for the rest of her life. When our Mother is raped, that way, the quality of all life begins to devolve. This is a negative experience injected into the Earth and the Creation.

The whites did a lot of experiments on us and they kidnapped many of us too. They brought some of our people back to Europe: a whole bunch of men that they took on a *peace mission* and the whites pretended they were dead, but it was not the case. Many

---

54. See note 1, page 18.

people don't like that story, but it is true. These men were not dead, the whites tried to make a stronger breed. They did the same with black slaves. These men were brought across the ocean to be studied and experimented on, and to impregnate white women in order to obtain stronger human beings and tougher men. That is what they did. No matter what your actions are, if they are terrible, they will be known one day or another, even after hundreds of years.

When the Treaty of the Two Row Wampum was made, it was between the traditional Mohawk people and the white men under the matrilineal identity of the Great Law of Peace. But today the government only recognizes the puppet regime of the band council who are not even Mohawk and do not respect the Mohawk tradition of matrilineal authority. Right now, we hear about them in the media, as they are still doing some dirty work. Actually, they negotiate with the government about a seigneury land claim, but they don't have the right to do that. They cannot negotiate our power.

We can draw many conclusions from these little stories, and there are so many things to say about my 82 years of experience that it would take months to tell about it.

When we speak, we speak the truth, and the Eagle Feather is there to prove it.

The Chief is selected by the women of the nation, and he wears the *kastowa* which sports deer antlers. Those antlers give him the ability to get and speak the truth. This is the reason why they give the Chief the *kastowa*: They recognize him as a person who carries the Good Mind.

Raymond Stone Iwaasa

Aiqne Maith
The Good Mind

Born in Alberta to a Japanese father who has worked with First Nations for most of his life and an English Canadian mother of Irish descent, I am Raymond Stone Iwaasa. I am under the protection of the Bear Clan. With my father, I met the Mohawk Traditional Council of Kahnawake in 1991, and I became its liaison agent for the Two Row Wampum in 2008.

I hold a PhD in Information and Communication Sciences from the Louis Pasteur University of Strasbourg. I became a lecturer at the Université du Québec in Montréal, and under the influence of Pierre Bourgault, my interest in the French language led me to produce two videos concerning the 1980 and 1995 referendums on sovereignty. I am driven by a strong concern for social justice, and am convinced that all North Americans—indeed, all the inhabitants of the planet—should recognize, find and accept their indigenous roots.

Today, in our society, I observe a large openness and recognition concerning the vital contribution women make to the balance of everything: family, society, nature and so on. This love, this energy that touches every element including men, allows me to live out, among other things, this experience of writing and sharing.

I believe that the Good Mind has permeated the land and the territory that we are invited to share and protect, indigenous with non-indigenous peoples. I dedicate myself to remaining open to others, to where I am, to my guests, visitors, parents, elders, youth, future generations and to all the elements. The Good Mind is not only native; it includes all humans and all that is alive.

My late mother had always wanted me to pay special attention to all beings: to peace and to women's protection while remaining attentive to the movements of the mind and spirit. She believed that I had received a lot from life, that my mixed Irish/Japanese roots were a gift, which prompts me to give a lot to others.

In 1991, when I first met the Myiow family in Kahnawake, my mother was still alive, following me and guiding me during my travels around the world (including France, Italy, United Kingdom, Mexico, Japan, etc.) Her humility and her capacity to welcome everyone were also well-anchored in the social actions and anti-racist struggles of my father. And my dad has always encouraged me to be open to the Good Mind, for myself and for others.

Even though my mother passed away in 2001 and my father and she had not been together since the 1970s, the inheritance from my parents helped me to open myself to the world. I believe that the Good Mind, or *Aigne Maith* in Irish (the language of my maternal ancestors), and the love of my mother still guide me and embrace me today.

For almost 30 years, my father and I have known the people of the Longhouse from the Mohawk Traditional Council of Kahnawake and their families. By frequently visiting them, we could understand that the respect they show and their *kahnikonnikonrhiio* (Good Mind) had surely been transmitted by the late wife of the elder Stuart, who departed in 1989. From this meeting onwards, we have always remained in touch and have evolved with each other no matter where we were in the world.

My father and I went to visit the *Kanienke'ha'ka* people, first in Kanesatake and then in Kahnawake, with an open heart full of love. In Kahnawake, we stopped at the jewellery and craft store of one of the eldest sons of the Myiow family, Keith. The tranquility of the moment allowed us to share and learn a lot.

Having worked with numerous Aboriginal people in Alberta and lived for years in one of their nations on Vancouver Island, my father was comfortable talking with Keith, who was peaceful and confident about the specificity of his nation. His people have a great deal of historical, geographical and contemporary knowledge, notably a familiarity with North American regions, particularly through specialized construction work (iron work) that male family members have practised, which led them to travel throughout the US, Canada, and even all around the world.

It was a chance but quite exceptional encounter, given our respective roots and the need to learn more about our civilizations and due especially to the fact that barely a year had passed since the Oka crisis[55]. The Canadian media painted the *Kanienke'ha'ka* people as a renegade warrior group not open to discussion and compromise rather than as a hospitable and peaceful people.

After an hour and a half of talking and procuring jewellery for our loved ones, Keith invited us to come back the next day to meet his father, Stuart Myiow Senior, and his younger brother, Stuart Junior. This would give us an opportunity to continue our exchange and grasp how the role of Stuart Senior's wife was paramount in their family and community.

At the second meeting, the addition of the elder accompanied by another son amplified the dynamism of sharing from the trio. We realized that our interaction had great potential and could meet several needs of learning and of teaching about our origins and our identities through the correction erroneous socio-historical information. We felt we would be able to counter racism, strengthen our families, and reduce isolation by sharing our respective networks by creating a link between west and east.

The father, Stuart Senior, mechanic, iron work foreman, Medicine Man of the Bear Clan, old defender of his nation against assimilation and neo-colonial interference, spoke in a very direct and honest way, which could seem at first to be a little rough for foreigners. He saw a very clear line between Aboriginals and the

---

55. See note 4, page 22.

others and said that mixed marriages end up hurting everyone, especially the children. For my part, I tried to make him understand that being born of a mixed marriage had been very beneficial to me. He also denounced the inability of the white man to act honestly with Natives because he is unable to give back the stolen land.

Nevertheless, he also spoke about the Good Mind and the good order of understanding, which interested me much because it seemed that neo-North Americans were living in rupture and denial of their identity, which was established upon the Aboriginal one. Indeed, most of the people I knew—professors, students, business innovators, among others—knew hardly anything about the history and culture of Native Americans. They did not even suspect that our attachment to freedom and to the Earth could come from indigenous peoples even if, for example, the US Constitution was largely inspired by the Great Law of Peace and Understanding that came from *Kanienke'ha'ka* people.

Stuart Senior insisted that the Good Mind allows us to verify and confirm all statements. Furthermore, vigilance requires each of us to consider how we present things and how the affirmations of all the speakers are understood; especially the people we have just met. He also evoked the notion of a collective spirit and collective consciousness that underpins the concepts of co-consciousness. This motivated me to share more with him and his people because I knew of some psychologists who were studying this phenomenon in Europe.

Furthermore, the elder took care to put us at ease. Besides, he and his people do not want, nor expect, that all those from the colonizing peoples to jump into boats and return to their continent of origin. On the contrary, we are clearly invited to work together to restore and respect the treaties and the sovereignty of territories by relearning history and cleaning up our political system.

When it was his turn to speak, Stuart Myiow Junior, from the Wolf Clan, the youngest son of four, showed great oratorical skills, an ability to communicate plainly, all the while demonstrating a good sense of humour. He was poised and spontaneous at the same time. Over the years, he has become spokesman for the Longhouse, and he had always been very close to his late mother.

Stuart Junior believed that, due to their continental origins, newcomers arrived impregnated with a way of thinking that was totally different from the people who welcomed them: mercantilism, expansionism, social persecution, domination by religious dogmas were all part of what shaped their thinking. All this had slowed, even stopped, their understanding of the nourishing earth where they landed. They didn't know how to protect it.

The understanding that Stuart was referring to was the foundation of the identity of individuals who populated the Americas at this time. They maintained a very intimate and living relationship with our Mother Earth by cyclical ceremonies of thanksgiving that recalled the essence of the laws of nature.

Stuart Junior, like his father through marriage, was called to assist a balanced female/male political power embodied by the Longhouse. This power is neither patriarchal nor matriarchal. Instead, we say it is matrilineal, as it comes from the women, but in a balance that removes domination between genders. The mother of Stuart Junior, the wife of Senior, was *Oianer* (Chief) and *Kanisentsera* (Wolf Clan Mother).

The matrilineal system has always helped the community to behave better, to define itself as human and to ensure the wellbeing of the Earth, of nation, and of all relations, including one's neighbours—even during times of occupation by them. Matrilineality patiently teaches the importance of peace between nations. It also instils in us that our collective survival depends largely on sustainable practices and balanced policies, thus supporting the fundamental role of women as much as men in society. According to the Great Law of Peace and Understanding, all women are mothers of nations, as they are intimately connected to the living Earth.

For *Kanienke'ha'ka* traditionalists, discussions take place in council where the whole group shares with each person speaking, which validates the statements made and gives a perception of the speaker's state of mind. A great advantage of this consensus process is that it eliminates differences and misunderstandings, protects the Good Mind in the group, and encourages a collective understanding. If we can agree on an issue, then we can close the subject, take action, and open discussion on the following subject. However, the discussion may be resumed later if necessary. To understand what a good "closure of the discussion" is a matter of common sense—and of the Good Mind. For all Aboriginal peoples and their descendants it is very important, traditionally, to reach the best consensus possible. It is sometimes necessary to temporarily close the discussion, leaving the subject to evolve over time, and reopen it later, always with the goal of achieving consensus.

Our Myiow family hosts' traditions have been sincere, peaceful and well-established for centuries, yet always adapted to modern life thanks to this protective constitution of the Earth and all its children: the Great Law of Peace and Understanding. Very open, skilled and experienced, with witty and sincere minds, Stuart Senior and Junior possess important spiritual, social and scientific knowledge. Protectors of truth and justice, they know how to demonstrate that their egalitarian traditional values respect the decision-making balance amongst genders and recognize treaties between nations. They could be a model for us all.

Did our occidental ancestors (Europeans) sense that the Good Mind could be found in the Americas? I think that, during the colonization period, the Chiefs of the First Nations believed that the set of values from different parts of the world advocated the same rights to the protection of life, regardless of the civilization, because they now shared the same continent. However, it would take a pact promising respect and non-interference between the peoples: the Two Row Wampum Treaty. This was proposed by the Myiow's ancestors to Europeans (Dutch) in the state of New York in 1616. These chiefs were wise and they saw far into the future because the situations that required inter-nation decisions at that time are still relevant today: whether they be a forest fire in 1616, or nuclear and oil pollution in 2015.

Unfortunately, the negative impact of European society on the lives of indigenous peoples has led to a widespread loss of human and ecological values in favour of finance, overconsumption and industrialization. So it seems that neither of the two spiritual institutions could counter this destructive rush—and all to the detriment of the healthy and peaceful Good Mind.

Respectful dialogue in the spirit of Two Row Wampum to try to eliminate corruption within our organizations is a challenge that would surely give us the opportunity to see if our respective institutions know how to reach true peace and remain in the collective Good Mind—all of this for the preservation of life and our Mother Earth either in Kahnawake, Montréal, Dublin, Tokyo or Vancouver!

Pursuing reciprocal relationships with the father and sons of the Myiow family has been simple. I recognized the *Kanienke'ha'ka* traditionalist people as an educated nation that welcomes newcomers sincerity—this despite what many others allege because of the confusion and controversy which characterized the Mohawk people due to the Oka crisis. And all Aboriginal people I have known have been my mentors.

People of the Longhouse have had time to gradually know my mind, as I did with theirs. I visited them regularly. We discussed our lives, our loves and the challenges of our respective societies. Thanks to the respect of both sides and our sincere communication, our meetings were reassuring and joyful. They were held in a pleasant family atmosphere that allowed us to open up to each other to renew the links between nations, genders, races and generations, without falling into a tourist or commercial ideology.

Gradually, with a collective spirit, we have catalyzed our energies and have taken action, including bringing our support to several environmental activist groups, first in the region, then in the rest of the country and also abroad. It could be a rural neighbour municipality, or the City of Montréal, which was concerned about water pollution, or the March of Peoples for Mother Earth, or the Assemblée nationale du Québec (Québec National Assembly), which expressed the urgency of getting out of the oil era. Along the way, many events and enriching meetings took place involving a great deal of sharing and teaching. Our peoples have finally joined together in cooperation without interference from either side, according to the agreement of the Wampum, and all this in the Good Mind.

Gently, the voice hitherto silent—but no less loving, carrying Creation of women from around the world, particularly the Aboriginal—prepared, slowly but surely, to be heard again.

The Earth keeps a record of each person's passage and, according to the location of our birth, she assigns to us an origin. By sharing a single territory, we pool our identities, which have the potential to become a common identity on the condition that we work together to protect our Mother Earth.

Finally, the minds of the inhabitants of different continents are maybe called upon, as simply as one good thing finds another, like osmosis in water which completes and unifies itself. That's the Good Mind.

Yvan Bombardier

Le Drapeau de la Famille
The Family Flag

I am Yvan Bombardier, son of Jacqueline Lambert, who is the daughter of Yvonne Maillé. As a Québécois, I am under the protection of the Wolf Clan. I was given many names, but the one I cherish most was given to me by Katsitenserio, my Mohawk brother, during our first Peace Mission on the St. Lawrence River: Rotetsens, which means "The Dreamer." And I work in order to fulfill my dreams.

I am the founder and the coordinator of the Drapeau de la Famille and the organizer and the founder of the Peace Mission on the St. Lawrence River. It is a great intercultural event for peace and reconciliation between peoples through symbolic gestures of reconciliation and for an enhancement of our united legacies. This 12-day journey brings women, men and children, *Kanienke'ha'ka*, Anishnabe, Innu, Atikamekw, Métis, Quebecers and newcomers together; all make the trip from Kahnawake to Québec City with *rabaskas* (12-place crafts) and canoes.

The Peace Mission provides an opportunity to live in community, to share, to attend beautiful festive and informative evenings, to participate in ceremonies and traditional councils, to discover new areas of the land, to meet people committed to protect the environment, to become familiar with the culture of indigenous traditions, and to pool together our efforts for a common goal: to celebrate our humanity.

The Good Mind reigns in the Peace Mission. Whenever we need something, it happens, because we are on the good path, and we cross others who are also on this path at the right time. Thus, when we do good deeds, we accept what must happen. *Do what you must, come what may.* It means providential encounters occur the moment we need them.

When we meet in Kahnawake for the departure, we all come from different backgrounds. Many meet for the first time, while some are more familiar with each other, as with the river. When we go on the Saint-Laurent for the first time, our paddles keep hitting one another. Some fear the elements around them, and have to face their fears and those of the others. Some have never paddled before on the river, others swim with little ease. With time, of us, quietly, pace ourselves, and the paddles stop hitting one another. We end up finding harmony on this journey.

This year, we crossed obstacles that we thought were impassable. We traveled great distances in record time, never duplicated at other Peace Missions, such as the crossing of Lac Saint-Pierre, an inland sea, right after the Sorel Islands—a large expanse of water where the St. Lawrence widens and becomes shallow. To cross this expanse in *rabaska* or canoe represents a test. If we are in the centre, in bad weather, we can see neither of the two banks nor our destination. In addition, when it is windy, the waves usually push us in the wrong direction, unless the wind is coming in behind us, but it rarely comes from the west. In the past, it has happened that we took 11 hours to cross it.

All together, with the will to go beyond ourselves, one challenge after another we go through the steps that lead us to our destination. All this is possible from the pooled efforts of everybody: That is Family.

Every morning before sailing, we offer tobacco to the river and we smudge. At our arrival in Québec City, we hold the Tree Planting ceremony on the battlefields of the Plains of Abraham. We plant a tree that symbolizes peace, where the war took place, where the Abenaki and Algonquin were leagued with the French against the Mohawk and the English. By planting a tree on the Plains of Abraham, we symbolically repair what has been broken.

The tree we plant evokes through its roots the grandmothers and grandfathers who guarantee the transmission of the tradition. The trunk represents the marriage in love of the father and the mother, an immutable law that unites the opposites in harmony, to give life to the branches, which represent our children. If we want these branches to flourish, we must remind each generation to protect and nurture our roots. Thus, we will ensure flowering branches that will give fruit in abundance. If we cut ourselves off from our roots, our branches will dry out and die. Finally, the foliage of the tree is our environment that protects and nourishes us.

On the Drapeau de la Famille, our emblem, the tree, is presented on a white cloth, the colour embodying peace that allows our families to grow tall, strong and proud.

The flag represents the universal family, all the children that our Mother Earth sustains and nourishes from the unicellularon: plants, insects, fish, birds, mammals, including humans. It symbolizes our relationship with Creation.

When the French came to Turtle Island (now known as the Americas) in their vast sailing ships, many people who jumped out of the boat took refuge in the forest. They lived with the Native people and learned their languages. They also learned to feed, to shelter, to heal and to live in groups. They participated in the ceremonies and rituals of the people who welcomed them.

Earlier, when Columbus arrived in Hispaniola (known as Haiti today), he was welcomed by indigenous people of the area. He described this meeting to the King of Spain:

> They shared with us, they gave us everything they had willingly. They took great pleasure in pleasing us; they are very gentle and without knowledge of what evil is, neither do they murder or steal. Your Highness may believe that around the world there can't be better people. They love their neighbours as themselves.

Consequently, the kings of Europe quickly appropriated the lands of these nations even if these lands were never ceded to them. They imposed their destructive knowledge and their wars upon indigenous peoples, often with the blessing of the Pope, the spiritual leader of these Catholic kings.

The Iroquois, for their part, have designed the first peace treaty presented to Europeans: the Two Row Wampum. The two rows represent the two parallel tracks where natives in canoes and refugees in their ships sail together on the same river without interfering, but always ready to help each other.

But unfortunately, our ships became like the *Titanic*. Several are blindly working in the engine rooms without seeing the horizon. Third-class passengers live in conditions worthy of the Third World, without seeing the outside either. Second-class passengers, the middle class, see the horizon through the portholes, and the rich have stunning views of the sea, without looking where they go, too obsessed by the joy of their luxury. The captain for his part leads the ship to disaster, concerned only about the company's image. Our identity, our cultures, our forests, our mountains, our rivers, and even our children that we send to wars are used as fuel in the engine room.

From their canoes, the echo of the grandmothers' complaint comes to our ears:

We cannot make our bark canoes anymore, for there are no more large trees. Our men cannot hunt because there is no more game. We can no longer fish because the fish are contaminated. We cannot drink our water because it is polluted.

The life balance of our Mother Earth has evolved from a way of perpetual renewal into a survival mode. We all have the responsibility to identify the source of the problem, the cause of these acts of destruction, so that we can achieve real change, confronting the real problems, and not be misled by the false solutions with which the governments of this world have us going around in circles.

We have become so dependent on the current system, for our comfort and our survival, that we have become powerless. We are unable to turn back. We fear that by ceasing to support this system, this threat to the system would also be a threat to our own survival.

This murderous behaviour towards our Mother Earth is the same behaviour that oppressed, raped and murdered women for tens of thousands of years. Yet, according to the Great Law of Peace, men must constantly work to liberate women from oppression and they must foster their leadership.

Even if the Great Law of Peace and the Two Row Wampum inspired the founding fathers of the US in their creation of the Declaration of Independence and the Constitution, these men omitted the role of women. The country then became a warlike nation rather than a peaceful one; an exploiter nation, rather than a preserver of sources of life. We must remember that male domination is not natural, but was created by a violent oppressive process toward women, through rape and murder, particularly in societies under the influence of religion.

To facilitate the peaceful transition to save our Mother Earth, indigenous authorities promote the return of the feminine authority and inner balance of masculine and feminine within us. Native American spirituality encourages us to restore the balance between women and men in order to repair the destruction we have caused.

Who would be cruel enough to want to kill his or her mother? Yet each one of us kills our Mother Earth and, by that very fact, we threaten all future generations because of the destructive things we do or allow to happen.

But that's not all. If I came to your place and threw you out of every room in the house, relegating you to the closet under the stairs, how would you feel? And if you talked too much and I shut the door to block out your voice? This is what is happening today on the reserves. Moreover, because the ceremonies were demonized, it was even forbidden for Native people to play their drums. This law fell in the late 1960s, but the evil of deculturation was already done.

Friends of mine live in the forest and see their trees cut. We are all responsible. We have to prevent these companies from destroying forests. Even in the most remote areas of the province, certain lake water is unfit for consumption because of residual contamination from mining, forestry exploitation and hydroelectric dams.

The Québec identity is defined by our belonging to the Earth and our awareness of this belonging. For me, my sense of belonging is linked to Montréal, where I was born; it is also related to the water flowing in my veins: the St. Lawrence—sacred water. We must realize how much we need to save water, and to recognize it as the way in which mothers carry us before giving birth; this water, which is also the blood of our Mother Earth.

We have been cut off from our roots. It is up to the true human being, the one that the Mohawks call the *onkuehón:we*, to define and build life. We have to remember that we are made up of the Earth and that we belong to her. This is what I learned from my contact with my Native brothers. If we had the consciousness that our grandmothers had, we would take care of our environment; we would reclaim our attachment to the Earth, rather than asphalt and trace the path of the pipelines.

Even if the reserve of Kahnawake is located near Montréal, across the Mercier Bridge, we have a great ignorance of its history, and especially of the people who occupied this region for thousands of years. The *Kahnienke'ha'ka* knew how to use the territory in the right way and how to exploit it in a balanced manner by perpetuating a healthy environment for future generations.

The current situation of Native peoples is not easy. Neither the provincial nor the federal governments help the situation. Decisions are made as if these peoples were not there. They see their forests suffer clear-cutting by logging companies, their rivers polluted by mining companies, and all under the federal jurisdiction. This is what justifies, for them and for us, the need to separate ourselves from the federal system but also from the capitalist system in which we live and which exploits the resources in a way that does not respect the Great Law of Peace. This whole economy is based on a war economy. Peace demands truth, justice, recognition and compensation for past mistakes and then forgiveness for them.

What our Mohawk friends present to us in their constitution is a way to unite. It is not enough to separate us from the current system, but we must unite with the Native peoples who are our roots. This fusion would make us a single large family whose members recognize, meet and celebrate diversity joyfully, accomplishing things together for our children, for the future, and by respecting the grandparents. This is the way we create a people.

Furthermore, the band council is a federal system that was imposed on Native peoples. This one is elected, which is not representative of Native traditions. It allows the federal government to have people in these communities to sign contracts with them—but paradoxically these people are also the employees of that government.

Traditional Council, for its part, keeps the traditions and history of the nation alive. Members of this council are very few, a consequence, among other things, of residential schools[56], which have extensively decultured Native peoples. The Traditional Council of Kahnawake's members are defending their culture and try as much as they can to keep it intact. They are pure traditionalists.

The band council is patriarchal while traditionalists advocate matrilineality, which means that women play a key role. With traditional Mohawks, there are as many women as men Chiefs, and it is women who choose men who become Chiefs, since they are able to recognize those who are brave and courageous, those who will defend them and their families. Moreover, grandmothers know how to recognize liars and cowards. It is their role to identify which men carry with them the truth. Among the Mohawks, women have the power of the veto; if a man does not respect his word, they push him out on the spot.

---

56. See note 20, page 86.

We have much to learn from the vision of Mohawk tradition-alists. If things worked according to their tradition in our society, we would have no politicians who lie to us: "From the minute you lied, you're out!" There are values, such as truth, we must learn to respect. Women are there to teach these values to their children. As men, we would do well to remember that, and we should take the time to listen to women, our mothers, those who know how to take care of us.

Unfortunately, many Mohawks have perverted their tradition by religion. The Catholic Church has even canonized a saint, generating religious tourism in Kahnawake, which has nothing to do with their own tradition.

In the past, during Full Moon nights, all the women gathered to receive the grandmothers' teachings. Now men are invited to attend the ceremony because we all need to relearn the basics of our education.

We must listen to the words of the elders before they disappear. These are pearls of wisdom. I am moved every time I hear them. They remind me of who I am: a proud Québecois. This is the way my roots grow, making me a Native. I love my land and I am ready to defend it, just like I am ready to defend my brothers and sisters who have lived on it for millennia. Only through this unity and peace will we be able to change the world.

Brian Sarwer-Foner

ERA
Ecological Response-Ability

I am Brian Sarwer-Foner, born in Montréal of Jewish origins. I am an environmentalist, social ecologist, multidisciplinary theorist and musician. In this chapter, I present the ERA project, which involves some ecological ethics aimed at inspiring concrete actions needed in order to achieve tangible results in terms of improving our Mother Earth's health and that of all life and all relations.

Perception is an important aspect of human existence; we all have different perceptions of different things: *individual* and *collective* perceptions. We could say that there are two very different ways to see the world and that they are both true. On that point, I want to acknowledge Grandfather Stuart Senior for talking about the truth, because truth is fundamental, but often it has two sides because we live in a paradoxical universe.

TRUTH 1: We live in a crazy and messed up time. Is there anything more insane than the fact that we are actually waging war against what keeps us alive? We don't care about our future generations. We are so selfish, so stupid, and so narrow-minded that we give all our confidence and devote our whole life to a corrupt, rotten system which sees only short-term profit for the benefit of the people at the top: the one percent. Everybody else is just a slave. We are destroying the living systems of the Earth and its biodiversity, we are impacting the climate system, we are spraying chemtrails in the sky, we are rape-mining the Earth, we are polluting the waters, and we are causing desertification and creating holes in the ozone layer. People are dying of cancer because of all the toxins in everything that we eat and drink. It is crazy and no one seems to care.

TRUTH 2: We are living in an amazing, exciting time. People are waking up! Not everybody, but at least some people organize incredible spiritual gatherings; people are getting together, they are connecting to Spirit, they are ready to listen to the First Nations, to listen to each other. There is some hope. We share the same vision of the type of world we would like to live in. There are plenty of possibilities. Solutions emerge and we learn how to apply them. I could go on and on . . .

Two opposites: both true.

We have so much knowledge and technology and we could talk about the evils of technology; there are certainly many, as much as there are positive sides of it. For example, take the Internet: We are being monitored by the corporate nation-state military system that invented it. Everybody is plugged in and disconnected from reality. Because we are now monitored, our private lives can be infiltrated. The powers can be informed, and they can know every step we are about to take. At the same time, the Internet is amazing. We can communicate with people all around the world. We can communicate with First Nations in Asia, Africa, Australia, and we can share our knowledge. We can come closer to having One Heart, One Mind. Both of these different realities are actually occurring here and now.

One thing is for sure: It is an amazing time to be alive. Nevertheless, alongside all this incredible potential, horror and tragedy are also present. We are living in a time of crisis, but for me, the central issue is the environmental one: the attack on our Mother Earth, the war we are waging against her.

So, what can be done? When we have gatherings, we talk about many things that are good. We start to approach and to understand each other so that there is room for teachings to come out and to be heard. This is great. We speak about plastic and water, about differences we can make as individuals. Some of these teachings are even related to the old ways, to the oral tradition that has been passed down through generations and generations. These teachings had been lost, but now they are coming back and need to be encouraged. This all fits into the ERA project. What is our potential as an individual? And what is it as a collective? This is where things get very interesting and deep.

I believe that an ecological caring crisis is going on in the world right now. Who cares? Who really, truly cares in their hearts about life on the planet? I know that many honestly care, but we are only a small subset of society. Nevertheless, we need to embrace this idea and keep it central. Anything that we bravely do will make a difference, even if we know that at the same time we are part of the problem. It is a fact: We are all a part of it. If you drive a car, sorry, but you are a part of it. I drive a car myself, so I am part of it.

Indeed, everything we do is still tied to the corrupt, sick system that has gone on so far that we are threatening the living structures of our planet. It is not to criticize ourselves; it is to identify exactly where and how we are trapped in order to find a way to free ourselves by taking our responsibilities.

If we want to live a pure life, we have to remove ourselves from society and live in the bush to become totally self-sufficient. Some Native people have never left nature, but sadly and tragically, they cannot keep doing so, because the environmental impacts are getting so great that these people cannot even live in their traditional territories and subsist anymore because the natural resources are becoming so depleted and damaged. I give reference to my Anishinabe friends who live just 300 kilometres north of Ottawa, in La Verendrye Park, and who are having their homes clear-cut right now, and this is within a wildlife reserve!

In order to reverse ecological irresponsibility, we are acting collectively. We need to look at the opposite: We need to become ecologically responsible. To change the whole world could seem idealistic, but we could start to do it through small individual actions, like not buying bottles of water. And then, by adding many other small changes, we will eventually come to a global change.

I heard Grandmother Francine talking a lot about our responsibility toward the water. Ecologically, we all have responsibilities: individual ones, and collective ones. But we all have a wonderful potential too that is well beyond the abilities we even know that we have and are capable of. We ought to realize this potential, learn new abilities, and respond with them.

The environmental crisis is a human crisis. If we continue to do our worst, we will deplete the ecological system and mess up the natural world so much that we could end up causing our own extinction. Life might take a million years or so to regenerate. In terms of the time span of our solar system, this is a blink of an eye, but of course, for us, it is tragic.

Why have humans become so sick that our denial allows our ecological irresponsibility to be maintained just so we can stay in our illusory comfort zone? Why? Because we have a man-made, faulty economic system that is constructed upon erroneous values that are driving the world to the detriment of the ecological system. Economy looks at ecology as an infinite resource, but it is not!

The first important word in the ERA Project is *Ecological*, and the other two are derived from the word: *Responsibility*. Now, if we break down the word Responsibility, we get *Response-Ability*. ERA: Ecological Response-Ability.

How would decisions be made? What would the political and economic systems look like, if ERA were at the centre of concern? All would be radically changed. ERA could, and even should, reach the governmental level because it applies to everything, and this includes the Two Row Wampum. Taking care of our Mother Earth would influence our brothers and our sisters because it would be an example of how people ought to behave. That is the way ERA works: leading by example until the new Ecologically Response-Able habits become the popular way to behave. Thereby, people would start to switch their thinking, and their perceptions. But the process is not complete until the actions accompany the thinking: ERA thinking and ERA actions!

We may believe that it is impossible to bring the world together, but we have had events in the past where many countries have come together: usually in sad situations and most often in times of war. Take World War II, for example, when a threat was clearly identified. The Nazis were trying to take control all over the world. The countries that did not want this to happen ignored their differences and came together because they had to address the emergency. So the industries, the economies, the politics, and the daily activities of the people were all focused upon and geared towards this war effort to stop the Nazis. And don't misunderstand me; I don't support war or violence, but this is a good example of how we can work together with attention and motivation. So, if parts of the world can come together for something like this, then why can't we work together to co-create a better world for future generations and stop the war we are waging on our Mother Earth?

I believe ERA is the answer that can shift people's thinking and centralize their actions. It could be applied to any positive project for environmental social change. For example, permaculture *is* Ecological Response-Ability in action. Another example involves country-sized parts of the oceans where bits of plastic form a floating layer that chokes life. There are four areas like this in the oceans; some are bigger than the US. So, a young Dutch man, Boyan Slatt, has invented a system of collecting the plastic in an efficient way by using bio-mimicry. He was 19 when he designed this. He now has a whole team of experts now working with him. Of course, a solution like this is not enough on its own. The cause of the problem has to be addressed too: We have to stop our addiction to plastic and stop producing and consuming it. This is ERA in action!

ERA is an idea that is in development, and its goal is to inspire people to start having councils about problems and to come up with the best solutions—many that are already here—and put them together. For example, we could have products promoted by ERA, such as composting toilets, permaculture and so on. ERA Communications could help popularize the solutions that make tangible differences; all of this achieved in a peaceful way.

I believe that addressing such a huge problem could be compared to a huge wheel that is stuck, but when you start pushing, it starts to turn. Once it is turning, a momentum is developed, and the wheel turns more, and more, and more. If we start to organize, to gather and really demand political change and boycott polluting industries, then we could change the world. We know what is needed. The government should only be implicated to manage things for the benefit of life and all relations, and the same goes for economics.

Back in the '60s, John Lennon and the Beatles wrote one of the most famous songs: *All You Need is Love*. We need to have love in our hearts; we need to care about what is around us. Love and caring are the same things. Late in his life, the great ocean explorer Jacques Cousteau said: "If you care about something, you automatically love; if you love something, you automatically want to protect it."

We need love for ourselves, for all of our relations within humanity, and all of our relations with the whole living world, which also includes the Spirit. We cannot just be talking about change; we need to co-create it. We still have not reached our potential, and we certainly have not yet assumed our responsibilities. Now, it is time for maturity, it is time that the seeds sewn in the '60s bear fruits 50 years later, and that the fruit bear new seeds, so later generations can enjoy life too, in an ecologically healthy world.

What would things look like if love was at the center of everything? What would society and law look like if politicians, economists, and corporate leaders had love in their hearts? It would look very different. Social and ecological justices would be at the centre, would automatically be the priority, if everything was based on love. We certainly would not allow corporations to continue to do what they are doing. They too would be obliged to have care and devotion for life and all relations so as to assume their Ecological Response-Abilities.

As humans, as a species, as children of our Mother Earth with this highest of consciousness, we have the responsibility to realize our maximun potential. We act like children who have not been taught the very basic rules. If you want to play, then clean up your mess after you have finished. But what we are doing is creating ever more of a monumental mess with new toys and new things to distract us from our duties.

We have to get our focus together and assume our Ecological Response-Abilities so every single action will nurture the collective power. That, in turn, will then be strong enough to make a real difference and eventually change the world, so that we can live in a new ERA, in balance with nature, while considering and caring for life and all relations, with both ecology and humanity flourishing within the heart of future generations.

Lucie Mainguy

Tout se transforme
Everything can be transformed

Passionate about aromatherapy and herbal remedies, I am a distiller and user of essential oils. In my opinion, no book can teach aromatherapy better than experiencing plants through smell. First of all, essential oils are aromatic substances that are messengers of plant wisdom. The aroma has the power to connect us directly to the plant in a spontaneous, intuitive and instinctive way, and it connects us to ourselves at the same time through the breath. The sense of smell, which can bring us a lot, is a sense that should be highlighted.

Initially, what fascinated me most about essential oils is the scientific aspect: their medicinal functions and their active molecules. I saw oils cure many things with very few adverse side effects and even some surprises: you cure one thing but heal two or three others at the same time without intending it. When we know how to heal ourselves, we become self-reliant, independent, confident, and aware that, the resource is there, thanks to the good care of Mother Nature. It is a way to heal with pleasure, using something natural and enjoyable. I do not know many people who fall in love with their medications, except for those who use essential oils.

During the tuberculosis epidemics, sanatoriums were often installed in coniferous forests, which have the power to help us overcome respiratory problems. Québec is very rich in this kind of aromatic substance, and we are not aware of it. Coniferous oils, when it comes to problems of lung function, should be used in diffusion to recreate the ambience of a forest. And what's even better is to combine the essential oil with hydrosol, which optimizes the feeling of the forest atmosphere. Hydrosol is condensed water vapour obtained by the distillation process when extracting oil; hydrosol and essential oils are the two halves of the message of the aromatic plant.

At first, when we start using the oils, we respond to a physical need in a medicinal way. Then, we realize that we love the oils and we enjoy using them, which satisfies the heart and the emotions. Furthermore, we realize that a certain energy is involved because our spiritual body is touched and stimulated by the vibration of the plant. So, the body, heart and mind are reached simultaneously, which provides general contentment.

The Ancient Egyptians were among the first humans to capture the aroma of plants. They seem to have developed this tradition inspired by China. The Arabs have perfected the technique. The alchemists, from whom we inherited the tradition, developed the distillation method that we use today. This practice synergizes the four elements in order to extract the fifth, ether—an impalpable substance manifested by life, that is to say, the mind. You could also say that smell is the most subtle of the physical bodies and the most physical of the subtle bodies. The alchemists, therefore, seek to capture this ethereal element of the living.

Breathing an essential oil means fusing with the spirit of the plant. However, if the oil is used in an olfactory way, our body knows how to protect us. When there is abuse, the nauseous feeling warns us that we've had enough. We have to listen to be able to perceive the signs and heed them. Furthermore, when the oils are ingested, some know-how is required. Where there is action, there may be a reaction . . .

In 1988, I founded Aliksir with the late Pierre Mainguy. That's how we started exploring the aromatic potential of Québec, one plant at a time, starting with conifers. When we distil, we collect and transform a large amount of plants from which we capture the aroma, and then we give back to the Earth any plant residue. The compost of our plants is given back to the soil that, when fertilized, generously produces again.

Through my work with plants, I developed an intimate relationship with our Mother Earth, and I am genuinely concerned about what we inflict on her in today's world. I am particularly concerned by a harmful typical habit of our society: the toilet flush. This little home comfort equipment (the toilet), now widespread, wastes plenty of drinkable water, pollutes rivers and deprives soils of tons of organic material produced by humans.

At home, 30 percent of our drinkable water goes directly into the toilet. With this simple gesture, we contribute to the asphyxiation of rivers every day, and to the pollution of groundwater and to soil degradation. The fatal error occurs when, six to eight times a day, we drop our excrement into the water.

There are things that it is better not to mix. This is the case of drinkable water and excrement. These two natural resources, each equally important, lose their value as soon as they are mixed. The *all-goes-to-sewer* system represents a huge volume that must be processed at expensive cost by water treatment plants, with results that are far from complete purification. Indeed, municipal sewers transport waste of many industries as well as traces of hormones and drugs that are released by the body into the toilet. These substances are not completely removed during the purification process, and end up in the water we drink.

Through the use of the toilet flush, we create a break in the natural cycle of organic material, and soils pay the price. The thin layer of soil that covers our planet is the basis of virtually all life on Earth. When soils are deteriorated, life on Earth, especially human life, is threatened. Giving back to Earth what it has given us is necessary to maintain balance and fertility.

In the past, the Amazon forest was densely populated. The pre-Columbian peoples who inhabited this region were able to support themselves through the rich soil. Analysis of thick black layers of humus that characterize some Amazonian sites indicated to researchers that this black soil, the *terra preta,* was created by man.

These people had developed an effective sanitary management and a productive and sustainable agriculture by composting systematically all their waste and excrement in combination with charcoal.

Why do we not preserve our drinkable water and why do we not benefit from the invaluable potential of human waste fertilizer, following the example of these people? The knowledge and technology exist to manage these organic materials. The solution is simple and economical: Just consider the widespread use of dry compost toilets. Other nations around the world have begun to do it, such as Sweden, Switzerland and Germany. Why not here?

In addition to the conservation of water and soil, the benefits of composting toilets are numerous. They reduce the costs associated with the production of drinkable water and wastewater treatment. They extend the life of disposal field wastewater while providing the raw material to obtain high quality compost. Besides, to prevent pollution certainly costs less than to have to treat it. Currently, Québec regulation allows the installation of dry toilets in exceptional cases only, since this system is considered to be an option of last resort.

By investing in research and development, I developed a model of toilet that flushes without water: a *dry-flush* . . . [57] To successfully develop such a project on a large-scale, we need to maintain the level of comfort of a flushable toilet. Now, with the model that we have created, we just turn the crank, which replaces the flush, and the droppings are covered by litter. We also manufacture and market a litter inspired by the *terra preta* of Amazon: a mixture of our plant residues from distillation, of charcoal and of thermophilic bacteria. We are far from an outhouse!

To facilitate the fair return to our Mother Earth, the system also includes a digester that replaces the septic tank and which produces black soil after composting. All this positively affects the ground and ensures perfect control of odours and pathogens. Indeed, the digester is bottom fed, so it ensures the process is odourless and without health risks. It empties without any intervention,

---

57. The project *Caca d'Or* (Golden Poop).

by means of overflow, after one year of retention. A total of five cubic metres initially provides two cubic metres of compost. Moreover, the heat generated by the composting phase is recoverable and can provide significant energy input. According to the volume of organic material managed, this heat can supply enough hot water for a residence, or provide complete self-sufficiency for heating a house, even against the harsh Québec winters.

We are all the authors of daily pollution when we send our excrement into the water. Yet the use of toilet flush is not a health necessity, nor an economic or an environmental one. It's a habit. To promote the use of dry compost toilets would leave our heirs with a healthier water and Earth.

Holly Dressel

Prescience of Native Thought

My name is Holly Dressel. I am a researcher, author, film-maker and professor at the McGill School of the Environment. I met the Myiows in 2002. When I learned about their Longhouse work, I had been an environmental journalist, filmmaker and activist for long enough to have made a key realization that I now try to inculcate in my students when I teach courses in environmental studies. That realization is:

If you care about the state of this planet's natural systems, about forests or water or species diversity or the oceans or the integrity of life—you must understand as much as you can about the belief systems and practices of the indigenous people where you live, whether those beliefs are long gone, or are still struggling to survive, as is so often the case here in Canada. If you want to spend your life as I did, trying to understand and defend natural systems, you will also end up working closely with Native people: because they got there first, and because they know how.

When I met with the people of the Longhouse, I had already been working with David Suzuki for over a decade. Thanks to our work with groups like the Cree in the sub-arctic and the Haïdas and other BC coastal nations, or from projects in India, West Africa and Central America, we knew that Native groups understand how humans should be living within nature far better than Western science does. By that I mean, they understand how human beings can support themselves within a natural system, like a forest or a desert or the shores of an ocean, and not overuse or despoil it.

Around this same time, our work took us to the Convention on Biological Diversity of the UN in Montréal, which has now recognized, through the Declaration on the Rights of Indigenous and Local Communities, the knowledge and wisdom of traditional ways of managing the Earth[58]. Parts of its precepts are recognizing that native people have lived in Canada for many thousands of years without destroying the base of their support. If we environmentalists and government resource managers want to learn how to do the same, we must spend some time sitting at their feet, listening.

I had had a farm in the Chateauguay Valley[59] for many years, and had familiarized myself with the traditions and beliefs of the people native to this area, especially the Kahnawake Mohawk, the *People of the Flint*, who my sources called the Iroquois. They live now confined to a reserve just south of the sprawling city of Montreal. I'd read about this group of people in books, written, for the most part, by educated white people— not by Mohawks. So when the opportunity came to work with Stuart Myiow Senior and Junior I was very happy. The Myiows had heard David Suzuki and me when we were interviewed on the local radio station and they invited me to one of their socials. This began the process of introducing me to Mohawk life in the 21st century, not the one I'd read about in books, it was an experience that has enriched my own life beyond anything I could possibly express.

Shortly after we met, I was approached by a grassroots citizens' group called the Coalition Rurale du Haut St-Laurent, and was told that a massive effort was being made by industrial hog farms to move into our valley. This extremely destructive and polluting

---

58. TEK, Traditional Environmental Knowledge
59. A city in the area of Kahnawake reserve.

industry had already literally killed eight rivers in southern Québec. The water situation in their central region, around St-Hyacinthe, was so dire that they had to expand to find new water sources, which of course they would then contaminate with the tons of liquid waste from their new CAFOs (Confined Animal Feeding Operations).

I found out that our small group, mostly Anglophone, was only one of dozens trying to defend water, land and property through all of rural Québec. None of these groups were in touch with one another; all were fighting bitter community battles in efforts to protect their property and surroundings from the smells and contamination from a massive, international industry.

At the time, Québec was the largest hog producer in North America, with more hogs than people. Most of the production was destined for export to the Far East. I felt we needed to warn the people of Kahnawake about this development, as their reserve sits in a swampy basin at the confluence of all the rivers that would receive the hog waste. Moreover, it incidentally is also the area of intake for Montréal's drinking water.

We had had to spend a good deal of time and trouble to explain the situation and our position to our own communities, both French and English, and we never managed to sufficiently galvanize our urban connections, because it seemed so separate from them. But in only a few sentences, our Mohawk friends instantly grasped what it would mean for us all to be downstream from such an industry.

We met with the Myiows and with Kahnawake Band Council members from their environment committee, but it was Stuart Junior who organized our groups. He inspired and helped us to understand timing, public relations and so many other aspects of an environmental campaign that our ad hoc groups of householders and farmers had not been able to grasp before. We worked together for four or five years. To my knowledge, this was the first time in Québec that grassroots citizens groups, both English and French, allied with a Native group to fight for an environmental cause.

We were massively successful. Trying to get environment min-
isters and governments to listen to us seemed to us to be an almost
hopeless situation. Nevertheless, we really did alert them to what
they called "social unrest" in the population regarding hog farms.
They first instituted minor (and to us completely inadequate) restrictions on the industry. Eventually the Parti Québécois put a
moratorium on hog farm expansion, but the Liberals rescinded this
under Environment Minister Tom Mulcair. That upset us very
much; but fortunately a good deal of damage to this industry had
already been done. Indeed, powerful hog exporters like Olymel
were outraged by any regulations at all, and had already begun to
move to Manitoba and the Prairies, and from there to Mexico and
the Philippines, where they continue to destroy land and water with
almost no restrictions. But our Valley was saved.

There were many other occasions on which the non-Natives
who worked with them benefited enormously from the deeply
spiritual, yet equally pragmatic, understanding of nature's basic
needs that the MTC (Mohawk Traditional Council) and its members understand so well. For example, the Myiows attended a sem-
inal conference called Rethinking Development in Nova Scotia in
2005. The country of Bhutan had sent a large delegation of digni-
taries and professionals. In two workshops and in private meetings,
Stuart Junior and his father introduced them to the foundational
concepts of the Great Law of Peace and the workings of the Traditional Confederation, and inspired them, almost to tears. The
Mohawk men described a society under female authority, in which
men do not lead into wars and expansion but serve and protect the
women, so that real community life may be enjoyed in peace. I
have since learned that many of these concepts found their way
into Bhutan's own new constitution.

In the winter of 2007, the newly-elected Prime Minister
Stephen Harper pulled the Canadian flag from the main ship of
what is arguably the most effective environmental protection group
in history: the Sea Shepherd Society. Its captain, Paul Watson, was
faced with heading out of an Australian port with no flag to protect
him. As soon as they heard, the MTC made him a flag of the Iro-

quois Confederacy to sail under. It still flies on the Sea Shepherd ship: the Farley Mowat, which prowls the southern Pacific every year protecting whales.

That following summer Paul Watson came to their Longhouse to accept a formal flag agreement that Stuart Jr had managed to broker from the other Confederacy nations. David Suzuki and I wrote about this day in the third book we did together, *More Good News*. We said there that the ocean is very big, and most of us feel very small and entirely inadequate to protect it, but the MTC did not see things that way; they simply knew that they had to do all they could. However small or inadequate it might seem, it was a lot better than doing nothing; and it turned out to be efficient. In the ensuing years, those ships, under their flag, have saved literally hundreds of whales from being killed by the Japanese navy.

That could be the motto of their efforts today; however, the MTC still fights nuclear proliferation; they still do everything they can to make Canadians understand what damage the residential school system[60] and the predation on native women continues to do to native people. They also do incredible outreach to French elementary school groups, introducing the children to Iroquois beliefs in school programs every year. In many cases, even the teachers, much less the children, barely realize this very proud and famous nation still exists, and that many of its members are still trying to keep their culture alive; so it is an exciting experience for all concerned. The MTC also participates in many festivals, lectures and conferences every single year.

I have never met a group of people, such as the Myiows themselves, who are more stubborn and as focused on the work they have to do. They are incredibly generous with their time and their personal lives. They have sacrificed so much of their own resources and interests in order to keep alive the traditional values and practices of their people, and trying so consistently to serve the needs of the Earth. I can't express how grateful I am for the opportunity

---

60. See note 20, page 86.

they have given me to attend their traditional ceremonies, to hear the old songs and see the dances, and also for the efforts they have all made to help me and many others to try to understand what humanity's place in the world needs to become.

While other belief systems teach us to pray to gods or saints or spirits for favours, protection, health and prosperity, this group, and in my experience, most other native groups in the world, do not ask the world for favours. In their ceremonies and in their lives, they instead *thank* the Universe, over and over, for being what it is. They thank the strawberry for being a strawberry, they are grateful to the winter, to the maple tree, for the turtles and the water and the insects and the fish . . . They appreciate what is, rather than what could be, or what they personally might want. It is a lesson I think all of humanity needs to learn, if we want to continue to live here. If we need to be convinced of that, I will add that the Great Law of Peace and their traditional ceremonies fit in with what science is beginning to understand about system complexity and what the laws of physics demand. Even the UN and many national governments (Canada, Kenya, India) are putting their remaining wilderness areas under the power and direction of their Native groups. I am so very grateful to the MTC for helping me and many others to begin to understand the prescience and continued relevance of Native thought.

Katsitenserio
Stuart Myiow Junior

Thia'teiohon'tsake Tho'nato'rohon
International Relationships

I have been honoured to serve the whales, dolphins, seals and all the other creatures on this Earth. Their beauty, intelligence, strength and spirit have inspired me. These beings have spoken to me, touched me, and I have been rewarded by friendship with many members of different species. If the whales survive and flourish, if the seals continue to live and give birth, and if I can contribute in ensuring their future prosperity, I will be forever happy.

CAPTAIN PAUL WATSON

I n June 2007, the Mohawk Traditional Council of Kahnawake had the honour to host Captain Paul Watson, Founder and President of the Sea Shepherd Conservation Society. The gathering was organized for the purpose of presenting the registry and the flag of the Five Nations to the Sea Shepherd for the ships *Robert Hunter* and *Farley Mowat*. We responded to the fact that the Canadian government had revoked the Canadian registry of the *Farley Mowat* due to economic pressure from the Japanese government. For this reason, the *Farley Mowat* was forced to take to sea in December of 2006 as an unflagged vessel. As such, they would have pirate status, meaning they could even get killed and they would have no legal defence. This, of course, would have been unacceptable to the entire world. The Sea Shepherd Conservation Society is the only organization on Earth that protects our oceans wildlife with such determination and love. We decided we should support their efforts and give them the protection of our flags. The presentation of the Mohawk flags for the *Robert Hunter* and the *Farley Mowat* is an historical event. Never before has there been a deep-sea, foreign-going ship flying under the colours of the Mohawk nation or any other indigenous Turtle Island sovereign nation. At this gathering, Captain Watson declared:

> "... *if we are going to save this planet we need to align ourselves with traditional communities that really care for the Earth and our Oceans. In our world today, governments represent corporations first, the voters second, and the environment last ... I was never proud of the Canadian flag but the Mohawk flag is one that I can be proud to sail under. We intend to bring the Mohawk colours to the far ends of the oceans to protect life and habitats for the future generations of all of our relations of all species.*"

Established in 1977, the Sea Shepherd Conservation Society is an international non-profit, marine wildlife conservation organization. Their mission is to end the destruction of habitat and slaughter of wildlife in the world's oceans in order to conserve and protect ecosystems and species. The Sea Shepherd uses innovative direct-action tactics to investigate, document and take action when necessary to expose and confront illegal activities on the high seas. By safeguarding the biodiversity of our delicately-balanced ocean ecosystems, the Sea Shepherd works to ensure their survival for future generations. I am really proud of facilitating the work of my good friend, Paul Watson. And I know that he appreciates the work we do, the same way that he knows that I appreciate the work that he does: He's my brother. As long as people remain my allies, they are my sisters and brothers; they become the best kind of friends. When I appreciate the work people do for our Mother Earth, I push them to the top, and I protect and defend them as well.

On June 20, 2014, in an unidentified Vermont location, we were honoured to attend the first annual general assembly of the Sea Shepherd, something we considered to be the most important gathering on the planet. It consisted of strategy planning for the year's missions and safety issues, and so on. This event had to take place in Vermont, as Captain Watson could not enter Canada because Stephen Harper took away his passport to placate the Japanese whalers. While traveling to the event, we found a freshly killed deer on the side of the road, which we considered to be a gift which marked the importance of this gathering.

The spirit of this deer reminds me and connects me to another important event in my life that ranks on the same level of importance.

In 1988, my cousin and I were traveling back to work in New York City, on the same road where I found three dead wolves in 1985. This time, we saw a deer which had been hit and was sitting in the middle of the road. It was very early in the morning, and we were on a three-lane highway. We parked and I told my cousin who was driving to back up. He did not want to because it was too dangerous, but I insisted and he obeyed.

When we stopped behind the deer, we saw that the animal's chin and neck were all raw and covered in blood, but the animal was still alive. We stood the deer up on its legs. The scared animal stumbled, trembling. I took the time to pet it: She was female. She looked at me and I could see in her eyes that she was crying. We walked to the guard rail where she stood for a while looking at me, then she went down the ravine where there was a fence. Once she got there, she stopped, turned around, paused and looked at me long enough for me to understand that she was communicating with me, and then she jumped over the fence even though she was injured.

This is one of the great experiences of my life; I don't care about anything else. I could have saved the world from burning; it does not matter. Saving that deer was one of the greatest things I have done. And among the great accomplishments of my life, the alliance we made with the Sea Shepherd Conservation Society is the greatest, and we are very proud of it.

Recently, we were invited to Ottawa by the Venezuelan ambassador to participate in a cultural event called *Alba*, which celebrates the trade agreement between Venezuela, Bolivia, Ecuador and El Salvador. We are the only ones who speak about matrilineality the way we do, and given where we are, we see people respond in different ways to the message we are transmitting. Quebecers respond a certain way, and when we go to Ontario, they respond in another way. Same as when we go across the US border, and so on. At the end of the Alba event, the women present were ecstatic to hear the message. However, all women respond according to the level of male dominance within their society. When people hear the message, they cannot deny what is said. I think that when things are going to change, first, we are going to see chaos, because people will have to leave the comfort of the status quo to go to something new. After a while, order will come out of this chaos.

Today, we cannot deny the evolution of the revolution; we cannot deny that change is underway. And I think the Latin-speaking world is in the process of opening their mind to the message we carry because the whole southern hemisphere is experiencing a feeling of sisterhood and brotherhood these days. Many of these countries are now making treaties among themselves to break out of damaging free-trade agreements with the US and Canada that are destroying South-American countries. When a country opens its doors and invites you in, then you have the opportunity to apply the medicine[61]. Even if we die today, as far as the message goes, we will have done what we had to do.

At the Alba event, I gave to the Venezuelan ambassador a package from the Sea Shepherd Conservation Society containing all the information Venezuela needs to know about the ships and the things that Sea Shepherd does in order to have Venezuela become

---

61. See note 1, page 18.

a friendly port for their ships. When ships of the Sea Shepherd travel all around the world, they don't settle for reaching a port just to find a place to stop. They enter the countries they visit, equipped with many kinds of resources to help to protect and defend marine life. So, once berthed, the Sea Shepherd crew reminds the country that a United Nations moratorium on whaling exists; they show how it is inhuman to practise shark and dolphin finning by showing shocking videos about these things, so people can see what it means to do such evil things. The Sea Shepherd Conservation Society is the only organization in this world that goes out and actually stops the slaughter of dolphins. Even Green Peace does not do this.

Paul Watson is no longer physically present on the Sea Shepherd Conservation Society ships, but the crews follow his example, keeping alive his spirit, his identity—it has become their identity now too. So, we do what we can to help those sailors to have the most peaceful battle possible. We want to help them wage peace against the enemy who is waging war against our beautiful Creation.

The thing Canada did to my brother Paul Watson by dropping his permit drove him down. There was no way we were going to allow such a thing to happen. This is why we stepped in and gave licenses to the Sea Shepherd Conservation Society. Because we allowed them to register their ships here, in Kahnawake, they painted *Kahnawake* on the back of those ships. So now, they sail around the world with the Five Nations Confederacy flags flying on their ships.

We have done what we could to help my brother who cannot fight on his own. He needs the help of as many people as possible in this world.

I would also like to point out that, even if I may not have spent much time with my brother Paul talking about our favourite things or the women we love, he is one of my greatest friends as well as being a protector of the Earth's oceans. He does for me what I cannot do for myself, and as I would do for him. So, I pay him tribute as we are both doing our jobs beneath the beautiful shinning face of our Grandmother Moon.

We are forever grateful for being able to assist the most important conservation society on the planet. We and all people of the Earth are indebted to the vision and fortitude of my friend Captain Paul Watson and the Sea Shepherd organization.

Niawen Kowa (thank you) for this fight which defends our Mother Earth, when almost everyone else is fighting against her. Stay strong and never give up. A Mohawk stays true and stands to the death, as does the Sea Shepherd: allied in the battle to defend our Mother Earth.

I never chose to fight the hunters of seals and whales. I never had the feeling of having a choice. I have seen what men are capable of doing on the floe. I've seen what they do on the high seas. I've been exposed to the horror. I have lived it in my flesh. I saw baby seals being carved up alive. I was struck by the ignorant brutes that kill the seals. I saw whales—beautiful, intelligent and self-aware—agonize endlessly. I heard them scream and die bathed in their blood . . . I'm in this fight to the end. I will never abdicate in front of the barbarians and bureaucrats. I think what we do is right and in the interest of our planet and our future . . . We will make the necessary sacrifices. We will go to prison. We will risk our ships and our lives. Giving up was never an option. It never came to my mind.

CAPTAIN PAUL WATSON

Tioronhiate
Grandfather Stuart Myiow

Wa'tenhoton'ne
Closing

One night, I was at home with my wife at supper time when somebody banged on our door. I opened it and asked the man standing there what the problem was. He told me that I was needed at the cookhouse, so I went there. People were going through great problems. I saw what was necessary: I had to take a walk by myself where my elders were buried when they first came to Kahnawake. So I took with me my bundle. That day was stormy; there was about three feet of snow all over.

On my way, I noticed a stick on the top of the snow. When I looked at this stick, my head started going round. I took it with me. I knew it was there for a reason, because the snow was too deep without covering this stick, and there were no tracks around; it was impossible that somebody had dropped it there.

I walked along the river down to the old cemetery. Once I got there, I lit my pipe, burned tobacco, giving thanks to it, and I gave thanks starting from within our Mother Earth, where all the spirits have been buried for years. I asked them all to come and listen to my voice and I gave thanks to them for coming.

Underneath the Earth, there were the roots of the medicines[62]. I gave thanks to them. Also, I gave thanks to all the medicines that

---

62. See note 1, page 18.

grow above our Mother Earth, including the trees that are useful. When they die, we use the dead wood to make our fires. And within the forest, there are the bigger animals: the deer, the moose, the bear, the wolf, the turtle, and so on. We also have the spirits of the animals that come to help us in the time of need. So I gave thanks also for all animal life, all insects, as they all provide life. Moreover, I gave thanks because we are all medicines, all gifts for each other.

I also gave thanks to the four winds who give us life. Sometimes, when the wind blows a certain way, we know that danger is coming. We have the lightning, the thunder; I gave thanks for them. There are also the waters that flow upon our Mother Earth. I gave thanks for those waters. Also, for the youngsters who follow us, I gave thanks for them, because they are learning to do what has to be done when the time comes.

When there is a need, the Creator creates what is needed. Sometime to encourage us to keep on going on the right path, the Turtle, the Wolf, and the Bear will present themselves in the clouds as they go by in the sky. That gives us strength to continue doing what is right. We invite the Creator to join us in our Thanksgiving Ceremonies, to dance with us. For all these things, I gave thanks.

This is the way I did the ceremony; then, I got answers. If there would not have been any sincerity in my words, then there would have been no answer. Everybody has to speak to the best of their ability to tell the truth. The Creator is not stupid. She gave us all life, and she knows when we speak if we are sincere. Without sincerity, there is nothing. Not many people understand these things today, even in my own people.

Hopefully, this book will have helped whoever reads these things to concentrate on what has to be done now. It is time to think about everything that you have read. I give thanks for this moment also.

EPILOGUE

Today was my penultimate visit to Kahnawake before submitting the manuscript to the publisher, and the Elder, Tioronhiate, proceeded with the closing of the book. We were both sitting in the shade of the big trees of the Longhouse on a splendid late summer day when he spoke. This moment is forever etched in my memory, and I will cherish it always. In his frankness and sincerity, with eyes closed, gathering tears in a handkerchief with one hand and holding my voice recorder near his mouth with the other hand, he opened wide his heart and spoke generously.

All the learning I did alongside the people I have worked with in Kahnawake has forged me. I learned a lot about them, but a lot more about myself. I contacted the Moon, the Sky, and the Earth as I had never done before in a simple, natural way—usually sitting by the Sacred Fire, or under the gaze of eagles, between our dives in the quarry where we swim.

This year I spent with them was the most formative and rewarding of all my life. I feel privileged to have been able to gather the precious pearls which allowed me to patiently string together this book—through each sharing, teaching, ceremony, dance, song, smile, tear, shared meal, through each welcome at my arrival, and each goodbye when it was time to go home.

I sincerely hope that anyone who reads this book opens themselves, even just a little, to allow the gentle Grandmother Moonlight to enter through that opening so that she cradles the heart of the ones who need kindness, so that she heals the wounds of those who are injured, so that she illuminates the road of those who seek their way, so that she reassures those who are frightened, so that she illuminates the nights of those who have dark thoughts, and so that she regenerates every broken fibre of femininity in each woman.

Women must absolutely recover their power. To do so, they do not need to become men, or to castrate them; they should instead look deep into the heart of their own identities and let that moment root so deeply that superficial events do not shake them. This is how the necessary forces they need to wisely exercise their power will be granted to them. Ho[63]!

GUYLAINE CLICHE

---

63. See note 2, page 136.

GLOSSARY

MOHAWK

Ahstawenserenhtha: One of the Chief titles of the Bear Clan

Aionwatha: One of the Chief titles of the Turtle Clan

Akweks: The Eagle, the Messenger of the Creator

Asen nikatarake: The three Universal Clans (Turtle, Wolf and Bear)

As'kànik'tshera: The hope

Astowakowa: The Dance of the Creator

Atonhetsera: True Spirit/Power

Atonwa: To give a name

Atotarho: One of the Nation Chiefs

Cayuga: One of the Iroquois Five Nations

Ie'iontate'rahkwa'kaias ion'kha'sotha: The Moon Assailed

Ie'karahkwa'ieri a'sonthen'ne: Full Moon Ceremony

Ie'ne:kwen'sinekens: Full Moon

Ieronhiakaiehronon: Sky Woman

Ionkiatishon: The Creator

Kanienke'ha'ka: Mohawk

Kaianerahsere'kó:wa ne skennen: The Great Law of Peace and Understanding

Kahna: Seed

Kanikonhiio: The Good Mind

Kahwatsei're a'aéiata'tiste: To Protect The Family

Kaneratentha: She drops the leaves (Tentha Cross' name)
Kanikonraksa: The Bad Mind
Kanisentsera: Mother of the Clan
Kanosesne: Longhouse
Kasotshesera: The Elder
Kastowa: The Headdress of the Chief
Katsitenserio: Pretty Bird (Stuart Myiow's Mohawk name)
Mohawk: One of the Iroquois Five Nations
Nia:wen: Thank you
Noh'naken:kha kowanen: The last Great Council
Ohenton Kariwatehkwen: The Words that come before all else
Oianer: Chief Woman
Okwaho: Wolf
Oneida: One of the Iroquois Five Nations
Onekora (Wampum): (abreviation of *wampumpeague*, an algonquin word) Belt made of pearls that carries a message. In the Great Law of Peace, each item of the Law is defined with a wampum
Onkwaneristha: Umbilical cord
Onkwehón:we: The True Beings
Onontake: One of the Iroquois Five Nations
Orenhre'ko:wa: One of the Chief titles of the Wolf Clan
Ratiniaton: The Turtle Clan (the Owners of the House, Fire Keepers of the Mohawk Nation and the verifiers)
Ronataion:ni: The Wolf Clan (those who lead the way)
Rorahkwaieshon: Grandmother Moon smiles upon him (Eshon Myiow's name, the son of Stuart Junior)
Rotetsens: The Dreamer (nickname givent to Yvan Bombardier by Stuart Junior)
Rotihskare:wake: The Bear Clan (those who deliberate, they preserve the knowledge of sacred medicine)
Sa'iontenekwenhsah'sats'te:ne: New Moon
Sarenho:wane: One of the Chief's titles of the Wolf Clan
Satekariwateh: One of the Chief's titles of the Turtle Clan
Seneca: One of the Five Iroquois Nations

Shoskoharo:wane: One of the Chief's titles of the Bear Clan

Taieh'wisats'teke tsinine iakon'kwe Kanienke'ha'ka: The resilience of a Mohawk woman

Taionterah'kwatahsawen: First Quarter (Moon)

Taiorah'kwen'hatie: Last Quarter (Moon)

Tehana'Karin:ne: One of the Chief titles of the Bear Clan

Teionhehkwen: One of the Chief titles of the Wolf Clan

Teio'rihwenton: Opening

Tekanawita: The Peace Maker

Tekarihoken: One of the Chief titles of the Turtle Clan

Tekenitehio hate: First treaty signed between indigenous and non-indigenous peoples in the 1600s (the Two Row Wampum)

Tioneratasekowa: Great White Pine, Great Tree of Peace

Tionkhiia:wis: She gives us

Tioronhiate: Bright Sky (name of Grandfather Stuart Senior Myiow)

Tsiioterahkwatehiaron'hatie: Grand Mother Moon Teaching

Tsiniia'wenhsere: The prophecy

Tsitewaterah'kwaketskwas kanhhóa: The Eastern Door

Wa'tenhoton'ne: Closing

INNU

Kepetan: The Path of the Ancestors

Maniteu-Ishkueu: The Woman Who Visits (name of Élyse Vollant)

Messinak Kassutasset: Persevering Turtle (name of Marie-Émilie Lacroix)

Nitassinan: Territory

Shaputuan: Big tent

Takunishishkueu: Medicine woman

Teueikan: Drum

Tshinashkumitin: Thank you

ALGONQUIN

Aki miskwi nibi wabo: Water, the Blood of Mother Earth

Aki Songideye Ikwe: Strong Hearted Woman Keeper of Mother Earth (name of Grandmother Francine Payer)

Aki Songideye Ikwe nin, mikinak dodem, Hull Nidonjabà, chi kokum anishanabe kwe: My name is Aki Songideye Ikwe. Born in Hull, I am Great-Grandmother Anishnabe, from the Turtle Clan.

Kichi-mìgwech Kichi-minido mìnwà nogoding: Great Spirit, Thank you for today

Matato: Sweat lodge

Migwetch: Thank you

Nibi wabo endayan Aki misqui: The water that I carry is the blood of Mother Earth

Poïgan: Sacred pipe

Tewehigan: Traditional drum

Wabo: Womb

KABYLE

Amazigh: Berber

Ddow lanaya: Under the protection of

Imazighen: Free men and women (those who inhabit Tamazgha)

Inebgawen n Rabbi: Those who are in need

Kahina: Witch

Takvaylit ghur warraw n tmurt: A Kabyle Woman in Native Land

Tafarka: Land ownership, Africa

Tafsut: Spring

Tafsut Imazighen: Berber spring

Tamazgha: Barbary

Tamurt n Iqvayliyen: The Kabyle's countries

Tanemmirt: Thank you

Tazekka: The great Kabyle house

Tin Ifsen: The Blossomed (name of Farida Zerar)

Yemma: Mamma

ZAPOTEC

Ba'dudxaapa'caxana: Woman giving birth

Nayeche': Thank you

IRISH
Aigne maith: The Good Mind
Go raibh maith agat: Thank you

BIBLIOGRAPHY

WEBSITES

Matt Gutman, Robert Rudman. "Venezuela's Mysterious Catatumbo Lightning Phenomenon Vanishes for Months, Then Reappears." *ABC News*. August 2, 2011. http://abcnews.go.com/International/venezuelas-mysterious-catatumbo-lightning-phenomenon-vanishes-months-reappears/story?id=14120203. Accessed March 1, 2016.

"About Us." *Aliksir*. www.aliksir.com/entreprise-aliksir.aspx. Accessed March 2, 2016.

"Helium-3 Mining on the Lunar Surface." *Esa*. www.esa.int/Our_Activities/Preparing_for_the_Future/Space_for_Earth/Energy/Helium-3_mining_on_the_lunar_surface. Accessed March 1, 2016.

"Le Drapeau de la Famille." *Famille du Monde*. www.famillesdumonde.org. Accessed March 1, 2016.

Frik Els. "China is taking lunar mining seriously." *Mining.com*. August 3, 2014. http://www.mining.com/china-is-taking-lunar-mining-seriously-65595. Accessed March 1, 2016.

"Mental Health and Wellness." *Health Canada*. January 27, 2015. http://www.hc-sc.gc.ca/fniah-spnia/promotion/mental/index-eng.php. Accessed March 1, 2016.

"Who We Are." *Sea Shepherd*. www.seashepherd.org/who-we-are. Accessed March 1, 2016.

BOOKS AND MAGAZINES

Myiow Junior, Stuart. *The Eagle's Cry*. Issue 7. Mohawk Council of Kahnawake. March 1994.

Myiow Junior, Stuart. *The Eagle's Cry*. Issue 9. Mohawk Council of Kahnawake. January 1995.

Emoto, Masaru. *Les messages cachés de l'eau*. Paris: Éditions Guy Trédaniel, 2004. 159.

Lacroix, Marie-Émilie. *La rivière des temps*. Lévis: Éditions de la Francophonie, 2012. 320.

TO REACH THE COLLABORATORS

MOHAWK TRADITIONAL COUNCIL OF KAHNAWAKE:
mohawktraditionalcouncil.net

Mohawk Traditional Council
P.O. Box 531
Kahnawake, Mohawk Territory
J0L 1B0

Marie-Émilie Lacroix: teuehikanish@hotmail.com
Grandmother Francine Payer: akiikwe.com
Élyse Vollant: vollant8@hotmail.com
Edith Mora Castelán: Contact the Mohawk Traditional Council
    of Kahnawake
Raymond Stone Iwaasa: hillofpeace@hotmail.com
Yvan Bombardier: famillesdumonde.org
Brian Sarwer-Foner: ERAcommunications.net
Lucie Mainguy: aliksir.com/img/Projet presentation
CACA D'OR d'Aliksir.pdf
Captain Paul Watson: Seashepherd.org

CONTENTS

ABOUT THE ARTISTS

Connie Marie Jacco and Krystal Myiow are both 29 and are single mothers struggling to survive and raise their children. As a young girl, Connie grew up in the Longhouse, learning the ceremonies, ways and culture of the Mohawk Traditional Council.

Krystal, the niece of Stuart Myiow Junior, spent part of her childhood in Kanesatake, the sister community of Kahnawake.

These artists embody the reality of young Aboriginal women today. They face oppression and demoralization with resilience, through their art.